THE ———
NEGRO
LEAGUES

THE NEGRO LEAGUES

40 Years of Black Professional Baseball
in Words and Pictures

DAVID CRAFT

CRESCENT BOOKS
NEW YORK • AVENEL, NEW JERSEY

A FRIEDMAN GROUP BOOK

This 1993 edition published by Crescent Books, distributed
by Outlet Book Company, Inc., a Random House Company,
40 Engelhard Avenue, Avenel, New Jersey 07001.

ISBN 0-517-07342-0

THE NEGRO LEAGUES
40 Years of Black Professional Baseball in Words and Pictures
was prepared and produced by
Michael Friedman Publishing Group, Inc.
15 West 26th Street
New York, New York 10010

Editor: Nathaniel Marunas
Art Director: Jeff Batzli
Designer: Kevin Ullrich
Layout: Charles Donahue
Photography Editor: Christopher C. Bain

Typeset by Classic Type, Inc.
Color separations by Bright Arts Pte. Ltd.
Printed and bound in the U.S.A.

8 7 6 5 4 3 2 1

Dedication

To the memory of D.B., a buddy from high school days who, by installing a glasspack on the exhaust system of my parents' 1967 Mercury Cougar, singlehandedly converted it to a wonderfully noisy "mean street machine" for the two of us in the summer of '68. Cruising over to our favorite burger joint, he and I talked about baseball and girls as the car radio blasted out the Rascals' "People Got To Be Free."

Acknowledgments

The author wishes to humbly thank the following persons for sharing their thoughts and recollections on the Negro Leagues: Saul Davis, Josh Gibson, Jr. (thanks for showing me the scrapbook of Josh Sr.), George Giles, Bob Motley, John "Buck" O'Neil, Ted "Double Duty" Radcliffe, Bobby Robinson, Bob Thurman, Armando Vazquez, and "Wild Bill" Wright.

And, though not directly quoted in these pages, other former Negro Leaguers—Ernie Banks, Jimmie Crutchfield, Bob Harvey, Monte Irvin, Lester Lockett, and Verdell Mathis—provided background information and anecdotal material as well when I spoke with them at a Negro Leaguers reunion in Chicago in 1991. Valuable information also was provided by Larry Lester and Don Motley of the Negro Leagues Baseball Museum in Kansas City.

Thank you, gentlemen, one and all.

Contents

A Few Warmup Tosses

The top salary for Jackie Robinson, who broke Major League Baseball's vile color barrier in 1947, was about $45,000 a year. If he were playing today, and putting up the same numbers he did at his peak—a .342 batting average, 124 runs batted in, 122 runs scored, 16 homers, 12 triples, 38 doubles, and 37 stolen bases—his pay would be comparable to that of several contemporary "marquee names."

Ernie Banks will forever be known as "Mr. Cub." But the title belies the fact that the shortstop-turned–first baseman terrorized big-league pitchers for two decades by socking 512 career homers and knocking in more than 1,600 runs.

When the dust settled after Willie Mays' twenty-two-year tear through the majors, his 660 home runs, more than 2,000 runs scored, and more than 1,900 runs batted in all contributed to his incredible .302 batting average.

Major League Baseball's all-time home run *and* RBI king, Hank Aaron, hit .305 lifetime while establishing more than a dozen other Major League or National League offensive records, including the highest number of bases obtained and the most years of scoring 100 runs or more.

Robinson, Banks, Mays, and Aaron share several common bonds, including their enshrinement in the National Baseball Hall of Fame in Cooperstown, New York. But many of today's fans, particularly young ones, are unaware that all four men began their professional baseball careers in the Negro Leagues—organized black baseball—just before entering the predominantly white domain of Major League Baseball.

It was the Negro Leagues where they honed their athletic skills, learned the game's nuances, and prepared themselves for stardom on America's big-league baseball diamonds.

This slugging foursome put up offensive numbers as dazzling as any of the black players who now grace the major leagues. Two other former Negro Leaguers, Monte Irvin and Satchel Paige, also are enshrined in the National Baseball Hall of Fame; this is based on the excellence of their play in the Negro Leagues rather than on their all-too-brief stints in the majors. Still other Hall of Famers, including Buck Leonard, Judy Johnson, John Henry Lloyd, Ray Dandridge, Josh Gibson, and Martin Dihigo, never played in the majors, but their high-caliber play in the Negro Leagues earned them reputations as some of the greatest ballplayers who have ever lived. And Rube Foster, "the Father of Black Baseball" and a major influence on all of organized baseball, was elected to the Hall of Fame—some fifty years after his death—for meritorious service to the game of baseball.

But this book isn't an argument for electing other former stars of the Negro Leagues to the Hall of Fame, though cases could be made for a great many of them, including a few (Ted Radcliffe and Jimmie Crutchfield, to name but two) who are still alive at this writing.

This book is about a group of remarkable human beings and their love for and contributions to the game of baseball. It's also about dignity, people's perceptions of race, and the price some have had to pay to earn a rightful place in the pages of baseball annals.

This book is about storytelling, too. A number of surviving members of the Negro Leagues contributed heavily to this work through their anecdotes and recollections. Some stories are wry and amusing, and others unavoidably downbeat. But

Classic stance by classy ballplayer: William Julius "Judy" Johnson was, arguably, the Negro Leagues' best all-around third baseman ever.

the gentlemen whose words are quoted in the following pages were there; they donned the uniforms, rode the buses, and put the leather on, or wood to, the cowhide in the Negro Leagues. They played professional baseball. Should you ever have the opportunity to meet and talk to a former Negro Leaguer, either in an intimate setting or as part of a larger discussion, do so. On one hand, these stories borrow from the universal language of the game: a triple to the gap and a peel around the bases; an eyeful of dirt on a diving stop of a grounder; and a leap off the bench when a teammate scores the winning run. On the other hand, though you won't experience the name recognition with them that you would with a Mantle, a Strawberry, or a Canseco, there is a unique and enduring richness to their stories.

In addition to the contributions the former players made to this book, the input and energy of several other people should also be noted here.

Larry Lester and Don Motley, treasurer/historian and execu-

tive director, respectively, of the Negro Leagues Baseball Museum in Kansas City, Missouri, offered their thoughts on many aspects of life in the Negro Leagues, as well as the important contributions of black professional baseball to the national pastime. They also provided me with access to some of the players quoted in this book and made arrangements with my publisher for many of the illustrations used herein. I could not have done this book without Larry and Don's help and guidance.

W. Lloyd Johnson, the museum's former executive director and a longtime official of the Society for American Baseball Research, was an encouraging voice when I first approached him about doing this book. Lloyd put me in touch with his successor at the museum. Whether it's the game's greats or today's skyrocketing player salaries that are on your mind, Lloyd will talk baseball with you at the drop of a Cracker Jacks box.

Two other gentlemen deserving of special mention are Richard Berg and Edward Schauder. Their enthusiasm and

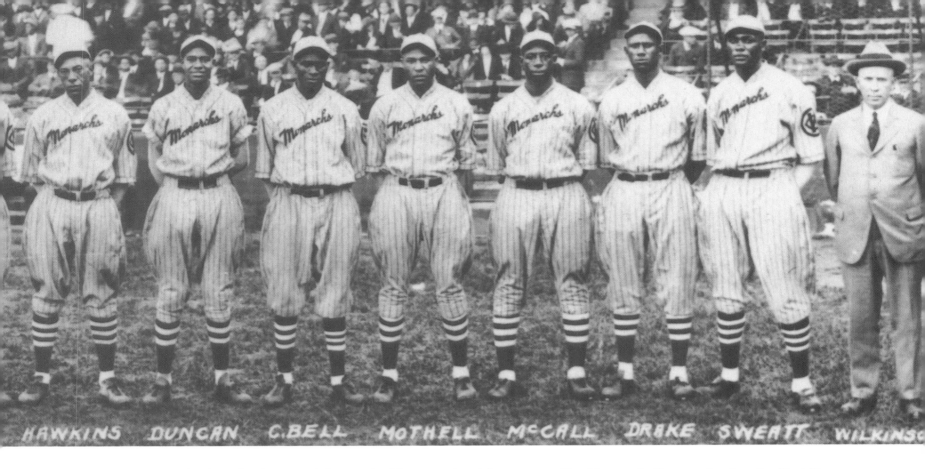

HAWKINS   DUNCAN   C.BELL   MOTHELL   McCALL   DRAKE   SWEATT   WILKINSO

their cooperation sparked my freelance articles on the Negro Leagues a few years ago. Richard and Ed established the Negro League Baseball Players Association (NLBPA), a nonprofit organization based in New York City. It is dedicated to help ease the financial burdens faced by most of its nearly 100 members, increase public awareness of the Negro Leagues and the contributions black professional ballplayers have made to baseball, encourage the National Baseball Hall of Fame and Museum to expand its exhibition of Negro Leagues memorabilia, gain corporate sponsorship for various activities (such as panel discussions), schedule private signings and public card show appearances, and offer authorized, limited-edition collectibles to fans all across the country. The NLBPA also supplied some of the photos used herein. (The addresses and telephone numbers for all of these organizations are listed at the back of this book.)

And finally, I would like to thank Karla Olson, editorial director of the Michael Friedman Publishing Group, Inc., for

The Kansas City Monarchs line up during the first Negro World Series in 1924. They beat the Hilldale club of Darby, Pennsylvania, five games to four (with one tie).

first approaching me about writing this book. It was Karla whose initial encouragement and ongoing support got me over the rough spots. This isn't the first book on the Negro Leagues and it won't be the last. But if it stirs you to investigate further the history of the players, coaches, managers, umpires, and owners who populated the Negro Leagues, then the book has served its purpose.

In their own fashion a few players pointed out to me—and correctly, I think—that the history of the Negro Leagues, while interesting in its own right as both baseball lore and as a remarkable period in black culture, is simply one more aspect, and an important one, of the history of the United States.

David Craft
Spring 1992

Chapter 1:

That Boy Don't Belong Here With Us

ud Fowler. Frank Grant. Fleet Walker. Weldy Walker. George Stovey. Sol White. Bob Higgins. Richard Johnson.

To the prejudiced and small-minded denizens of the national sports scene one hundred years ago, these extremely talented men were known as "darkies," "coons," "niggers"; some of their white-skinned teammates and fans were "progressive" enough to call them "Negroes" or "colored boys."

My son, if you aspire to be a servant of the Lord, prepare yourself for testing. Set a straight course and keep to it, and do not be dismayed in the face of adversity.

—Ecclesiastes 2:1–2

To those of us who are a century removed from the pain, hurt, disrespect, and violent confrontations these men experienced because of their color, they are remembered as pioneers whose frontier was organized baseball. They were professional ballplayers.

Blacks competed in the game, just as whites did, before, during, and immediately after the Civil War. Teams made up entirely of black players, though rare, did exist by the late 1860s. It was during this time, the period of Reconstruction (1865–1877), that the dual issue of racial equality and the integration of the nation's fledgling professional clubs was fielded cleanly by the National Association of Base Ball Players (NABBP)—and quickly dropped.

In establishing its organizational rules, the NABBP denied an application submitted by an all-black team from the East. White organizers went a step further by barring all blacks from participating in the newly formed league. By doing so now, they reasoned, they would avoid any possible discord among owners in the future because there would be no "colored persons" to create an uncomfortable situation for the owners.

African Americans, hopeful of better, fairer times with the passage of the Thirteenth Amendment to the Constitution in 1865, found themselves freed of slavery but bound by new "rules" that essentially kept them from enjoying the same opportunities as those enjoyed by white Americans; these double standards were at the core of Jim Crow America. Typical of the whole of American society after the Civil War, organized baseball didn't entrench itself in written restrictions so much as it fumbled along with double-talk, so-called gentlemen's agreements, and a policy of simply looking the other way whenever segregation reared its ugly head.

Opposite page: Slugging shortstop John Henry Lloyd was dubbed "the black Honus Wagner," a comparison Wagner considered flattering to himself. Lloyd's greatest following, despite an impressive batting average, came years later as a school custodian whom children idolized.

Above: Moses Fleetwood Walker (seated at left, with arms folded) and brother Weldy (standing, back row) both saw action behind the plate and in the outfield with the 1884 Toledo club in the American Association. The American Association was recognized as a major league, thereby making "Fleet" the first black American major leaguer. Opposite page: Adrian "Cap" Anson was a hard-nosed ballplayer and hard-hearted individual whose racial bigotry helped keep big-league baseball lily white for sixty years.

By the late 1870s, organized baseball—that is to say, white baseball at the major and minor league levels—viewed black players as persona non grata. These early leagues generally frowned on the signing of "colored players." A few team owners attempted to integrate the national pastime in the 1880s, but resentment by a majority of white players and fans undermined these efforts.

Indeed, historians have uncovered several documented cases in which black players' white teammates would refuse to take the field unless management benched the black players in favor of whites. In some cases, white players insisted that their team's owner drop black players from the squad altogether.

If a black player's uniformed brethren were so hostile toward him, imagine what he got from the hooting, snarling brutes on the opposing bench and from the spiteful cranks in the bleachers.

Death threats—oral and written—were commonplace in the lives of these black men who wanted but two things: respect and the same opportunities enjoyed by their white counterparts to earn a living playing the game they loved. In its simplest form baseball is a game played between two lines by two "nines," but back then any proud black man courageous enough to take his position on the baseball diamond quickly realized it was seventeen men against one.

Irish-born Tony Mullane hurled over 30 wins in five consecutive years in professional ball. He also hurled epithets at those he detested, which included catcher Moses Fleetwood "Fleet" Walker, the first black major league ballplayer.

Like Mullane, the Ohio-born Walker was a multiposition player. But unlike Mullane, Walker was a black man, and the first to play in the major leagues. Despite Mullane's grudging approval of his battery mate's defensive abilities, the fiery

Multiposition player John Beckwith won batting titles and home-run crowns during a career that spanned three decades and nearly a dozen teams.

Outstanding curveball pitcher John Donaldson played much of his pro career with the Kansas City Monarchs, the team he is credited with naming.

Observers called shortstop Dick Lundy, who had the range of Ozzie Smith and the throwing arm of Shawon Dunston, heir apparent to "Pop" Lloyd.

Irishman ignored Walker's signals behind the plate, choosing instead to pitch whatever he wanted regardless of the count or the score.

Walker's most celebrated nemesis, however, was Adrian "Cap" Anson. The Marshalltown, Iowa, native was a strict disciplinarian who went on to become the first ballplayer to collect more than 3,000 hits. Respected by many for his talents and feared by others for his way with his fists, Anson was a known racist. Several times throughout his career he was in the middle of a controversy over whether his team, the Chicago White Stockings of the National League, would take the field against an integrated team.

In 1884 a scheduled exhibition game between Anson's White Stockings and Toledo (of the rival American Association) nearly died at the ticket gate when player-manager Anson announced he would cancel the contest if Walker took the field. The irony of the whole shameful episode was that the injured Walker was not penciled in to start. Toledo manager Charlie Morton, miffed at Anson's bullying tactics, put Walker into the game anyway, and no further crises were reported.

Anson was more successful a few years later in his monomaniacal effort to keep blacks out of baseball. For a time in the late 1880s, George Stovey was one of professional baseball's top pitchers. He also happened to be black. And that made him a target for Anson.

In 1887, the hard-throwing Stovey was forging a superb 33-win season for the Newark Eagles in the International League and earning praise from even ardent critics of integrated ball when a midsummer exhibition game pitting Newark against Anson's Chicago White Stockings drew near.

Once again Anson threatened to pull his team off the field if a colored ballplayer took part in the contest. This time the bluff worked. It was said at the time that Stovey did not take the mound that day because he had told his manager he was ill. Later, however, the truth was learned, and another sorry incident smudged Anson's shining career.

Integrated teams were not the only ones plagued by racial scenes. Even when an all-white team was scheduled to play an all-black team, cries of protest pierced the air. In September of 1887—almost two months to the day after Anson's threatened boycott of the game in Newark—a game between the American Association's St. Louis Browns, an all-white team, and the all-black Cuban Giants from New York State, was nixed when several Browns players pressured team owner Chris Von der Ahe into canceling the game. The official line was that the Browns were riddled with injuries. The Cuban Giants knew better.

Integrated teams encountered the ugliest conditions. In 1887 in the International League, Buffalo infielder Frank Grant was greeted by choruses of racial epithets from a hostile Toronto crowd. It was just one in a series of such episodes.

Along with the taunts and the more subtle racial barriers he had to face in his brief pro career, the plucky second baseman dodged hundreds of pitches fired at his head and danced around the threatening spikes of base runners who literally flung themselves at his unprotected legs.

Like Grant, teenage pitching sensation Bob Higgins suffered the indignity of his teammates' refusal to pose with him for a team picture. Disgusted with the situation, manager Joe Simmons confronted one of the men, Doug Crothers. An argument broke out, Crothers socked his manager, and Simmons retaliated by suspending Crothers for several games.

In about a year's time Higgins faced such intense bigotry—probably as much from members of his own team as from opponents—that he threatened to quit the Syracuse club. By 1889 Higgins was out of organized baseball.

Richard Johnson was another black pathfinder. He had brief stints as a catcher-outfielder in a couple of minor leagues in the late 1880s, and hit close to .300 for Zanesville one year. But Johnson was out of professional baseball by 1890, another victim of white prejudice and indifference.

Weldy Walker was the younger brother of Fleet Walker. He appeared briefly for Toledo, his brother's team, in 1884.

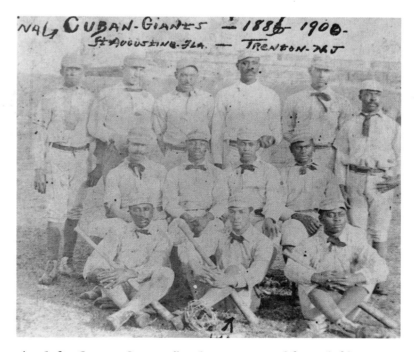

Ace lefty George Stovey (back row, second from left) was among the first blacks to play in organized baseball. In the 1887 International League he won 33 games for a fourth-place Newark club.

The club folded after its only season in the American Association, however, and the Walker brothers joined the ranks of the "unemployable" black players forced out of the majors by bigotry.

A few, including Fleet Walker, continued to play baseball at the minor league level. But their days were numbered. About the time of the Anson-Stovey incident in Newark in 1887, International League team owners met to consider the growing tension surrounding the race issue in organized ball. The ten owners narrowly passed a resolution that stated they would no longer draw up contracts with black ballplayers. The "color line" was now official.

Black players graced organized baseball with their presence on white teams well into the 1890s, but only in isolated cases.

Integration was dead.

All-black teams of the period, however, were gaining some measure of acceptance in the country's myriad of minor leagues. A few of these clubs excelled, though briefly, during their turns in organized ball. One year the Cuban Giants, for example, won nearly 60 games and lost fewer than 20. The team would later boast its league's leading hitter, infielder George Williams. He flirted briefly with the magical .400 mark before closing out the 1890 season with an eye-popping .391 batting average.

One problem faced by all ball clubs back then—white as well as black—was the financial instability of the teams and of the leagues themselves. The professional game, particularly at the minor league level, might just as well have earned the dubious title of "disorganized baseball." Teams came and went, often disbanding after a season or two. Others merged to form new teams. Entire leagues folded before their seasons ended. Players jumped one sinking ship only to find themselves adrift with another.

By 1898 the last traces of black players in organized baseball could be found in the Pennsylvania Iron and Oil League. The Acme Colored Giants, with an anemic won-lost percentage of .163, shut down operations in midseason.

With that team's demise, a turbulent, maddening period in organized baseball had finally given way to a slightly calmer but racially segregated period in which only whites could play at the minor and major league levels. Black athletes, despite their red-blooded forays into a predominantly white

The St. Louis Browns refused to play the East Coast–based Cuban Giants (opposite page) in an 1887 exhibition match.

Illustration © Mark Chiarello

Satchel Paige combined brains, talent, showmanship, and a love for the game.

Series of Firsts

Dan Bankhead and Satchel Paige were the first black Americans to pitch in the majors—Bankhead in 1947 with the Brooklyn Dodgers and Paige in 1948 with the Cleveland Indians. The duo is notable for other firsts, as well: Bankhead was the first black pitcher to appear in a World Series game (albeit as a pinch-runner), and Paige was the first black pitcher to pitch in a World Series game (he took the mound for two thirds of an inning in relief). Another Dodger, Joe Black, was the first African American to start and win a World Series game.

"workplace" over a twenty-five-year span, were now exiled to obscure semi-pro leagues and barnstorming tours to play in small towns across the country. The few times that all-black teams faced all-white teams after that came in the form of exhibition games.

Humor and theatricality were sometimes used to promote these contests. For example, near the turn of the century Bud Fowler and his All-American Black Tourists entered ballparks dressed in top hat and tails and carrying silk umbrellas. They then proceeded to trounce the competition. But how many observers were aware that the man leading this doubly talented troupe was professional baseball's first black player? Fowler contributed his pitching, hitting, and fielding mastery to a variety of pro and semi-pro teams throughout the United States and Canada over a span of three decades before taking his Tourists on the road with him for a last hurrah.

Another pioneer, Sol White, not only played on integrated teams in the late 1880s but later played, coached, and managed for many all-black teams. He was also a writer and a social critic. He penned the first account of the early black players' experiences in *The History of Colored Base Ball.*

White was adamant in his belief that the day would come when both races would enjoy equal footing on the fields of organized baseball, notably at the major league level. Some forty years after his book appeared, White's lifelong wish for racial equality finally arrived in the form of Jackie Robinson.

But black baseball developed and even thrived in the years leading up to Robinson's historic debut with the Brooklyn Dodgers in 1947. Smart, talented players, many of whom matched or beat the best efforts of their white counterparts in head-to-head competition during barnstorming tours or in exhibition games, forged an important entry in the history of baseball.

Their feats are legendary. Their names, to a majority of baseball fans, are not.

One name in particular stands out: Andrew "Rube" Foster, the "Father of Black Baseball." He was a superb pitcher and capable hitter in the early 1900s.

Foster is best remembered, however, for his organizational efforts, business acumen, managerial genius, and generosity. Without him, there may not have been the Negro Leagues as we know them.

Andrew Foster was nicknamed "Rube" after he outdueled fabled white pitcher George "Rube" Waddell, but Foster's contributions to the game of baseball went far beyond athletic excellence.

Often at the center of controversy, John "Bud" Fowler is credited as the first African American to play professional baseball. Although he never made the majors, Fowler's lengthy career took him all over the country, playing various positions for many teams. This photo is from 1885; Keokuk was part of the Western League. Fowler later assembled several clubs of his own that barnstormed the U.S. in the 1880s and 1890s.

Chapter 2:
The Spark

ost baseball fans with a sense of the game's history know that 1919 was the year that members of the Chicago White Sox conspired with gamblers to throw the World Series.

The scandal rocked the sports world and ultimately resulted in the creation of the game's most powerful position, commissioner of baseball. And while Kenesaw Mountain Landis, the man who held that office for the first twenty-five years of its existence, did nothing to spur the integration of blacks into organized baseball, his successor, Albert Benjamin "Happy" Chandler, did. Chandler backed the decision by Brooklyn Dodger president and general manager Branch Rickey to bring Jackie Robinson to the big leagues in 1947.

Two other events took place in 1919 that hold just as much significance to baseball—Robinson's birth and the birth of an idea: the Negro National League (NNL).

The maestro who conducted the historic debut in 1920 of black professional baseball's first truly successful league was Andrew Foster.

Foster's importance to baseball transcends the Negro Leagues. The man created an environment in which talented black baseball players learned to play the game using their smarts as well as their skills. He even mixed into this winning brew a few doses of psychological subterfuge.

One of Foster's players on the Chicago American Giants, Saul Davis, says that his mentor instructed them to verbally "rattle those one or two players" on each opposing team who seemed timid. "If we knew their pitcher or one of their infielders couldn't take it, if one of us got on base we'd call time and walk halfway over to that player and say, 'Where the hell'd you learn to pitch? You stink.' Or, we'd say, 'You better be watchin' for me when the ball's hit, 'cause I'm comin' right for ya.' We didn't really mean nothin' by it, 'cause we respected the other players, but we learned how to get on 'em, make 'em jumpy out there. Make 'em make mistakes. We used to say stuff to the umpires, too, to keep 'em on their toes."

Although Foster died several years before the majors' color barrier came crashing down, it was his Negro National League that served as the stamping grounds of future big leaguers

> *The first thing he did was open a drawer and pull out his bottle—but I refused his liquor. Even if I drank, I wasn't gonna let him know it…but I was a young ballplayer, and I knew he was only testin' me. He just laughed and said, "How you gettin' along here in Chicago?" Jock always looked out for us.*
>
> **—Saul Davis,** recounting an early visit with Andrew "Rube" Foster, the man the players lovingly called "Jock"

Opposite page: Rube Foster was a visionary who founded and nurtured the Negro National League. He died several years before Jackie Robinson broke the majors' color line in 1947, but Foster's influence on the game is still felt, even today.

Larry Doby, Monte Irvin, Hank Aaron, Roy Campanella, Willie Mays, Ernie Banks, and others, including Jackie Robinson.

Born in 1879 in Calvert, Texas (located east of Temple, along modern-day Highway 14), Foster was a preacher's son who quit school after the eighth grade and ran off to Fort Worth. A sensitive, religious youngster, Foster dived headlong into baseball—his first and greatest love.

By his late teens he was pitching for a regional barnstorming unit called the Yellow Jackets. By his early twenties he was talented enough to be invited to face big-league hitters in spring training competition. Legend has it that shortly after the turn of the century, the fireballing Foster earned the nickname "Rube" when he outpitched Philadelphia Athletics' ace (and future Hall of Famer) George "Rube" Waddell by a score of 5–2.

Another story passed down through the years involves New York Giants manager John McGraw and his ace hurler, Christy Mathewson. Like the Foster versus Waddell legend, this one can't be found in the record books or in the respective biographies of the principal characters, and it remains one of baseball's great "what ifs." Anyway, it has been said that McGraw was so impressed with Foster after seeing the black star in action one day that he either asked or hired Foster to teach his screwball to several members of the Giants' pitching staff.

As author John B. Holway wrote in his book *Blackball Stars*, "Whether the legend is true or not, Matty suddenly jumped from 14 wins in 1902 to 34 in 1903; ["Iron Joe"]

Dave "Gentleman Dave" Malarcher was one of black professional baseball's more important figures in the 1920s and 1930s. Not only was he a talented third baseman, he was also a brilliant strategist. In 1926 he succeeded Rube Foster as the Chicago American Giants' skipper.

The Philadelphia Giants of the early 1900s featured Rube Foster (standing, second from left), historian Sol White (wearing bowler), and Charlie Grant (standing, far right), whom big-league manager John McGraw once tried to pass off as an American Indian.

McGinnity also won over 30 for the first time in his life, and the Giants leaped from last place to second."

Foster himself is reported to have had awesome seasons of as many as 40 and 50 wins against fewer than 10 losses each year. (He may not have been the best black pitcher of his time, either. An easygoing giant, Joe Williams—nicknamed "Smokey" Joe—may have earned that distinction. His fastball was legendary. In addition to amassing huge strikeout totals in single games and over the course of a season, Williams won more games than he lost in head-to-head competition with white major league aces. Still, Foster has to be considered one of his generation's greatest pitchers.)

Foster's playing days continued well into his late thirties, but by that time he had been serving as player-manager for

Saul Davis
1923

Quincy T. Trouppe

Ted Double Duty Radcliffe

Edsall Big Walker

Joe Black

Max Manning

several years. His knowledge of the game was immense. He is credited with inventing the bunt-and-run play, whereby a fast runner on first takes off with the pitch. As the third baseman runs in to scoop up the bunted ball and fire it to first to nail the batter hustling down the line, the other runner rounds second and, without breaking stride, heads toward the unguarded bag at third.

Judging talent was another Foster specialty. One can count among his protégés such great black baseball stars as slugging center fielder Oscar Charleston, John Henry Lloyd (whom the white Hall of Fame shortstop Honus Wagner called his equal), star third baseman Dave Malarcher, and outstanding defensive catcher Bruce Petway (who is credited with throwing out the speedy Ty Cobb twice in an exhibition game). The aforementioned Smokey Joe Williams was another brilliant player Foster took under his wing.

A top pitcher. A decent hitter. A fearless competitor. A master tactician. A shrewd judge of talent. A motivator. Rube Foster was all of these things and more. His greatest impact on the game of baseball, however, came in the form of organizational skills and business sense.

Foster facilitated a meeting of owners of the stronger, more successful black ball clubs at a Kansas City YMCA in mid-February 1920. For several months prior to this gathering, Foster had carefully considered his plan for an organized league of black teams. At the historic meeting, the group forged a constitution that prohibited the raiding of other teams for

What talent they had! Clockwise, from upper left: Infielder extraordinaire Saul Davis; multiposition player Quincy Trouppe, who later managed; pitcher/catcher Ted "Double Duty" Radcliffe; pitcher Max Manning; pitcher Joe Black, who went on to win fame with the Brooklyn Dodgers; and pitcher Edsall "Big" Walker.

players, and copied the white major leagues' reserve clause binding a player to his original club until that club determined otherwise.

This meeting was the birth of the National Association of Colored Professional Baseball Clubs, which would later become known as the Negro National League.

Eight clubs made up the new league. Among them were teams based in Chicago, Dayton, Detroit, Indianapolis, and St. Louis. Foster himself owned the Chicago American Giants. All of the teams were owned by blacks except the Kansas City Monarchs. That team was owned by a white man, J. L. Wilkinson.

Not only was Wilkinson named the new league's secretary, but he is credited with introducing to the NNL a portable lighting system that helped keep black professional baseball a going concern through the toughest of economic times.

The native of Des Moines, Iowa, worked closely with an Omaha firm to develop the system, which revolutionized the sport of baseball and now serves to underscore the innovative thinking that became the hallmark of the Negro Leagues throughout its rich history. The portable system debuted in the spring of 1930, a full five years before Cincinnati's Crosley Field hosted the first night game in the major leagues.

Wilkinson by that time had already earned the respect of his players and fellow owners. He made it a habit to travel with his Monarchs clubs on road trips, and often ate and slept in the same places as his players did. Like his friend and business associate, Rube Foster, Wilkinson was generous with his ballplayers, often advancing them part of their salaries when they needed money.

Years before he owned the Monarchs, Wilkinson owned the fabled All-Nations team. That barnstorming assembly, originally based in Des Moines (Wilkinson moved it to Kansas

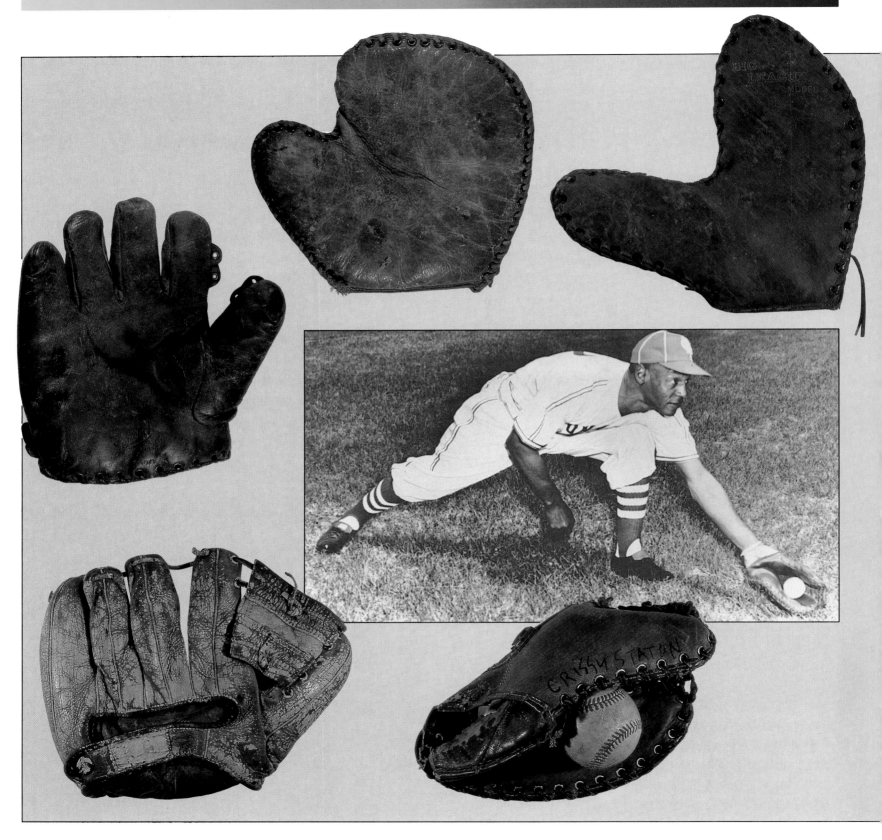

Opposite page: John "Buck" O'Neil could "pick it" at first base, a position he played for many years with the Kansas City Monarchs; O'Neil eventually managed the club. An excellent judge of talent and character, O'Neil later served as a big-league scout and ultimately became Major League Baseball's first black coach, working for the Chicago Cubs. Above: John House, of the St. Louis Stars.

City during World War I), included blacks, whites, Hispanics, Native Americans, and Asians, and once boasted the likes of pitchers Jose Mendez, the "Black Matty" (named for Giants ace Christy Mathewson), and John Donaldson, an outstanding southpaw who later pitched for the Monarchs and numerous other Negro League teams before serving as a major league scout in the Chicago area.

Nonetheless, the fledgling league was still Rube Foster's baby, and he cared for it like a proud new father. Despite the recurring problems of scheduling and rescheduling games, as well as facing the economic woes that plagued virtually all of the franchises at one time or another, Foster's leadership and personal finances kept the league intact and spirits up.

Foster made sure the players were well paid, that they played their games in better ballparks than their nineteenth-century predecessors, that contracts were honored on both sides of the bargaining table, that games were extensively promoted, and that the member ball clubs themselves were given whatever additional financial assistance he could muster.

For all of this Foster demanded, and got, the respect and support of the other club owners. His six-year rule was akin to a benevolent dictatorship. From its inaugural season in 1920 until 1926, when mental illness forced Foster to be institutionalized, the Negro National League and Rube Foster were synonymous.

In the beginning, at least, the league was fairly successful. Attendance was generally good. Gate receipts in 1923, for example, totaled nearly $200,000—not a great sum, but not bad, either, for an organization that lacked the white major leagues' traditional economic base and widespread fan support.

Late that same year a second league of all-black professional baseball teams got under way. The Eastern Colored League

"Crutch in the Clutch"

One would think that a ball club boasting such sluggers as Oscar Charleston, Sam Bankhead, William "Judy" Johnson, James "Cool Papa" Bell, and Josh Gibson would have little room for a spray hitter by the name of Jimmie Crutchfield. But it was Gibson himself who first referred to his speedy teammate on the 1935 Pittsburgh Crawfords as "Crutch in the Clutch." Nowhere was that truer than in East-West All-Star Game competition. In the 1935 midsummer classic, Crutchfield made a heart-stopping, barehanded catch of a ball hit by Philadelphia Stars catcher Biz Mackey with men on base that proved crucial to the West squad's 11–8, extra-inning victory. A year earlier, Jimmie fired a tremendous cannon shot from deep in right field to nip Chicago American Giants first baseman Mule Suttles at home plate. That throw preserved Satchel Paige's 1–0 win for the East squad.

(ECL), like the Negro National League several years before it, enjoyed solid support in its first season of operation. But the new league soon cast a buccaneer's eye toward its older counterpart and began raiding it of many key players with promises of higher wages if they jumped ship and signed with more affluent ECL teams in New York, Philadelphia, Baltimore, Brooklyn, and New Jersey. Most of the ECL teams were owned by white businessmen.

In 1924 a war ensued, bad blood flowed between the two regional superpowers, and Foster's plan for a nationwide association of black teams was trampled underfoot. Even worse, perhaps, was the fact that a couple of NNL teams were decimated when many of their players left to join teams in the Eastern Colored League. The Indianapolis ABCs actually dropped out of the NNL because it had lost so many players. (The franchise would later reappear in the Southern Negro League.) An uneasy truce was finally reached later that year, but the two leagues were virtually at odds with each other throughout their stormy history together.

Also at this time a third Negro League was created, this one in the South. Because of the economic climate in that region, the Southern Negro League, on the whole, never quite enjoyed the following or financial security of the NNL and ECL— and the latter two weren't without problems of their own.

The sensitive issue of players jumping from one team to another within the same league, or from the NNL to the ECL, was only one of the headaches for Foster and his group. Umpiring in the NNL, a task often performed by local whites hired on a per-game basis, was inconsistent at best. Also, some of the players and coaches resented the presence of white umpires on the field. Poor umpiring by blacks also drew the wrath of the players, coaches, and fans. In time, however, more and better black umpires called the games.

Bob Motley, a longtime umpire in the Negro Leagues who would later officiate in the Triple-A Pacific Coast League, stands at center stage as opposing managers Buck O'Neil, left, and Oscar Charleston, right, prepare to outmaneuver each other.

(Two top-notch Negro League umps who went places were Bob Motley and Emmett Ashford. Both saw action in the Triple-A Pacific Coast League, and in 1966 Ashford became the first black major league umpire.)

Perhaps the most vexing problem facing Foster and his fellow owners involved league schedules. Few teams in the Negro Leagues owned their own ballparks, so club owners frequently were forced to make expensive financial arrangements with unsympathetic white businessmen in order to have a "home" ballpark.

Sometimes, the teams afforded themselves the luxury of playing their games in minor league or even major league stadiums.

According to historian Robert Peterson, in his book *Only the Ball Was White*, the Cuban Stars leased Redland Field in Cincinnati for $4,000 in 1921. Thus, the Stars made history

This photo of owner Rube Foster and his Chicago American Giants was probably taken around 1920, the inaugural season of the Negro National League. Over the years, the Giants—like most black professional teams—pitted their talents against a myriad of pro and semipro teams, and barnstormed against white major leaguers.

"as the first Negro club to become a regular tenant of a big-league team."

Of course, regardless of whether its landlord was a club owner in organized baseball or the owner of an independent semi-pro team made up of lumberjacks or factory workers, each black club in this predicament of having no ballpark of its own had to make sure games were played when the white "landlord" team was out of town. Situations would arise where clubs zigged and zagged all over a region simply in order to get its games in and get out of town.

If one of the Negro League teams was a no-show, or if bad weather forced cancellation of a game or a series of games, it became virtually impossible to reschedule the matchup in the host ballpark later in the season. One team might play half as many games as another in the same league. This created a touchy situation for organized black baseball, particularly at season's end, when officials tried to determine which team was to be declared league champion.

Further aggravating the scheduling process was the fact that clubs occasionally elected to skip a league game in order to play elsewhere against another team, black or white, whose backers promised a larger take of the gate receipts. This was particularly attractive to those franchises that struggled week after week to meet their payrolls.

Yet, through all of the tough times and recurring problems his Negro National League encountered, Rube Foster kept it going, often using his own money to help a team with its travel expenses, player salaries, or equipment costs. He may have been an owner of the Chicago American Giants and therefore in competition with the other franchises in the league that he had created, but he wanted the entire league to succeed and prosper.

His direct association with player development was just as important. Foster called on his knowledge of the game, the subtle nuances and little tricks that he had learned from others or invented himself over the years, to teach his young charges how to play baseball with their brains and creativity as well as their brawn. Many players idolized him, and what he taught them about baseball and sportsmanship served them well as they competed against one another or against white teams.

Foster meant everything to the overall success of his league and to the individual successes of its players.

So, it was doubly sad when Foster began to show signs of strain in 1926. Strange behavior, ranging from nonsensical utterings to childlike actions, from paranoia to forgetfulness, compelled family members to move him to a Kankakee, Illinois, mental institution.

Ninety-one-year-old Saul Davis, who played for Foster's Chicago American Giants and who knew the great man well, recalls with sadness an incident that typifies the waning years of their leader.

"The first I heard anything about Jock's illness was in the middle of the summer, 1926," Davis says. "We were in the club room and Harry Jeffries was our captain then. Some of us were sittin' around talkin' and he comes up and says, 'We got to go out and see Jock after the game Sunday.'

"When we asked him what was the matter, he said, 'Well, they don't know. He's sick.' And when Jeffries told us where they'd taken Jock, I thought, well, you don't take sick people there. You take crazy people there. Charlie Williams said, 'Don't talk so much, Saul. Let's just get out there after the game an' see how he's doin'.'

"Well, when we got out there we saw it was a long walk from the grounds to the main building. We started walkin' and stopped dead in our tracks. There was Jock, sittin' in a kids' swing, just by himself, sort of starin' straight ahead and slowly movin' back and forth.

"Bill Foster [Jock's half brother] and Jeffries, our captain, went over there, I remember, but the rest of us didn't. We just stayed put. In fact, they didn't *want* us to go over there to him. And that was the last time I saw Jock. It hurt to see him like that because he was always so full of life. He was wise, and he had a great sense of humor.

"He was a great, great man, as far as I'm concerned. If you would do what he wanted you to do—that is, play ball his way, the smart way, and put your heart and soul into the game of baseball, then he was with you. But if you couldn't perform the way he wanted, he wouldn't fool with you. He demanded a lot, but he had a big heart. He was generous. He watched out for his players."

Foster died at the mental institution on December 9, 1930, at the age of fifty-one. Days later thousands of mourners attended his funeral in Chicago. The large turnout at the funeral was a testimony to the importance of this great man.

The Father of Black Baseball, the man who sparked a lasting interest in organized black professional baseball and prepared black players for the day when they might enter the white major leagues, was gone, and the world he helped create was about to come crumbling down.

Chapter 3:
The New Neighbors Down The Street

With Rube Foster gone from the scene, the Eastern Colored League disbanded, and the Great Depression tightening its choke hold on the entire country, black baseball limped along in the early 1930s.

Attendance was well down from the organized black leagues' heyday. Owners, even some white owners, found it tougher and tougher to pay decent salaries to their players, and the players found it tougher and tougher to make ends meet. And so, less than a year after Foster died in an Illinois mental institution, his beloved Negro National League—which had changed the face of organized baseball—packed it in, a victim of the times.

For black ballplayers it appeared that league play—even with its ongoing problems of scheduling, finding good umpires, and players disregarding signed contracts—was defunct. What would become of the many talented black men itching to take the field?

The emergence of independent teams is what saved the day for many of the players and kept black baseball alive during the depression.

The Homestead Grays and the Crawfords in Pittsburgh, the Elite Giants in Baltimore, the Black Yankees in New York, and the Monarchs in Kansas City came to symbolize the new order in black professional baseball. Successful and powerful, these clubs drew enthusiastic crowds wherever they played and featured some of the greatest baseball players, black or white, that the game has ever produced.

My first recollection of baseball is when I played catch with my dad and some of the other grown men in the area. I could tell it kind of pleased them, to see a youngster take such an interest in the game.
—Buck O'Neil, former first base standout with the Kansas City Monarchs and the major leagues' first black coach

By the mid-1930s, Josh Gibson, "Cool Papa" Bell, "Judy" Johnson, Martin Dihigo, Satchel Paige, and Buck Leonard were starring for their respective clubs. All of these men are enshrined in the National Baseball Hall of Fame in Cooperstown, New York.

Even with incomplete data on their career accomplishments, those stats that have been uncovered—combined with eyewitness accounts of the players' exploits against one another and against white all-star teams—provide us with a clear idea that these men were as smart and as talented as they come. Had there been no racial barrier in organized baseball during their prime years, they and numerous other black players would have starred in the big leagues alongside Lou Gehrig, Lefty Grove, Jimmie Foxx, Mel Ott, Dizzy Dean,

Opposite page: Josh Gibson gradually became a top-rank catcher, but he could always knock a baseball into the next county. Tales of Gibson's eye-popping home-run blasts always brought comparisons to Babe Ruth.

Outspoken, witty, smart, and energetic Effa Manley (right), along with husband Abe, owned the Newark Eagles. Her run-ins with players and fellow owners are legendary, and she raked Major League Baseball over the coals for its dealings with Negro League team owners in acquiring black players. Manley was a high-profile civil rights advocate as early as the 1930s.

There were times when he could make it from first to third on a bunt, or score from second on a fly ball to the outfield. "Cool Papa" Bell (below) was the most feared base stealer/base runner in the history of the Negro Leagues, the prototype for such future big leaguers as Maury Wills, Lou Brock, and Rickey Henderson.

Originally a semipro team, the Pittsburgh Crawford Colored Giants—the "Crawfords"—quickly became a professional powerhouse. At various times it boasted such luminaries as Judy Johnson, "Cool Papa" Bell, Josh Gibson, Jimmie Crutchfield, Satchel Paige, Ted Radcliffe, and Oscar Charleston.

Carl Hubbell, Bob Feller, and other white players of the era. Many whites, in fact, publicly affirmed the talents of their black counterparts. Dean, and later Feller, were particularly impressed by Paige. The cunning, charismatic Paige engaged in many a battle with his white peers before sellout crowds on various barnstorming tours in the 1930s and 1940s.

And if barnstorming was a large piece of the Negro Leagues' mosaic in the Roaring Twenties and postwar 1940s, it was virtually the whole pattern in the early 1930s. Surviving NNL franchise the Monarchs, with white owner J. L. Wilkinson at the helm, and the Homestead Grays, owned by former basketball star Cumberland Posey, Jr., were two of the independent teams that hit the road to find fame and fortune. Other inde-

pendent teams, or "indies," such as the Pittsburgh Crawfords, also established themselves as dominant black ball clubs that barnstormed their way through the Great Depression.

But by 1933, Gus Greenlee, a black Pittsburgh numbers racketeer who had built an expensive ballpark for his Crawfords and then named it after himself, changed all that.

That was the year Greenlee formed the second Negro National League. His fellow owners, Cuban immigrant Alex Pompez and blacks Tom Wilson, Ed Semler, Ed Bolden, and Abe Manley, also had made their fortunes in gambling and other illegal endeavors.

Manley's wife, Effa, though not involved in the seamier side of her husband's business affairs, was arguably the real power behind the couple's Newark franchise. According to historian Donn Rogosin, Effa oversaw the club's public relations and business affairs, and was not shy about player-management confrontations. She was active in civil rights issues, too, and after Jackie Robinson's debut with the Dodgers in 1947 she harshly criticized Major League Baseball for plucking the top talent from the Negro Leagues without proper compensation. She rightly claimed that this practice further weakened the black clubs' already tenuous financial situations.

The Grays did not affiliate themselves with the new league. Posey, their owner, while not engaged in racketeering, was forced to make a crooked black banker, Rufus "Sonnyman" Jackson, his partner in order to compete financially with Greenlee's big-money juggernaut.

This second NNL lasted well beyond the 1930s, but Greenlee's leadership—and the legendary Crawfords—did not.

Acting on tips from Greenlee's enemies, law enforcement authorities brought the curtains down on the racketeer's operations. The Crawfords' owner was unable to pay his players the top salaries to which they'd become accustomed, so they scattered to more profitable climes in the United States, South America, and Mexico. Greenlee Field was razed in 1939, and years later the site was used for a housing project.

Posey had problems of his own during the 1930s. In addition to the devastating effect Greenlee's raids had on the Grays' talent pool, Posey's financial situation was threatened by his floundering second team in Detroit. The Wolves folded after just one season. And Posey's partner in the Grays, the hard-living Sonnyman Jackson, embarrassed the dignified Posey with his public peccadilloes, including a near-fatal brush with extortionists and FBI agents in the streets of Pittsburgh.

Still, Posey continued to operate his beloved Grays and, once Greenlee was pretty much out of the picture, was able to

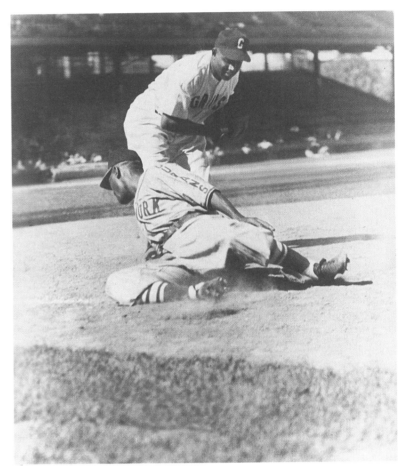

Above: First baseman Walter "Buck" Leonard slaps the leather on a New York Cubans player, 1946. Opposite page: All-Star competition made teammates of traditional foes.

put together a crack unit of ballplayers that dominated organized black baseball almost to the moment Jackie Robinson donned his Dodger uniform in 1947.

From the late 1930s through the mid-1940s, Posey's teams won nine consecutive Negro National League pennants. Those nine league championships began with the team's move to Washington, D.C. Posey alternated the Grays' home games between Pittsburgh and the nation's capital.

Also making headlines in 1937 was the creation of the Negro American League. The Kansas City Monarchs' J. L.

Wilkinson and several other white owners were instrumental in organizing the league, which also boasted teams in Atlanta, Birmingham, Chicago, Jacksonville, Memphis, and St. Louis. Organized black baseball once again sported two leagues. That rekindled interest in the nearly forgotten Negro League World Series of the past that had pitted two league champions against each other.

Enthusiasm for the annual series failed to match that for black baseball's other crown jewel, the East-West All-Star Game, which was the brainchild of Gus Greenlee. Like Major League Baseball's All-Star Game, the Negro Leagues' All-Star Game began in 1933 in the city of Chicago. (Comiskey Park,

site of the first Major League All-Star Game, was also the permanent site of the Negro Leagues' East-West contest for most of the Leagues' history.)

The country's black newspapers polled their readers to help determine which players would make the two squads—starters and backups. Each year hundreds of thousands of fans voted for their favorites, and tens of thousands of them attended the midsummer classic.

There were several reasons why the Negro League World Series never gained the status of the East-West All-Star Game. To begin with, the black World Series was baseball's version of a movable feast. As Negro Leagues researcher Larry Lester

The East squad's Pat Patterson smacks a foul ball off the West squad's Theolic Smith during the 1939 East-West All-Star Game, which the West squad won 4–2. The catcher is Larry Brown.

points out, blacks of the period had neither the disposable income nor the free time necessary to support a best-of-seven or a best-of-nine series.

In an effort to generate widespread interest in the Negro League World Series, promoters devised a plan to have the series' two combatants travel to cities other than their own to showcase the event for as many fans as possible. But to cover their travel expenses and still turn a modest profit, the two teams sometimes scheduled what actually amounted to exhibition games. These games had no bearing on the outcome of the series, and in the eyes of many, diluted the importance of the autumnal event.

Lester also points to the nagging problem of unbalanced regular-season schedules as another factor affecting World Series play. "Fans and writers asked how one team could be

declared a league champion simply because it played more games than its nearest competitor," Lester says. "The second-place team often sported a higher winning percentage."

The East-West All-Star Game, then, was the highlight of the season for the players and their fans. To begin with, the fans had the greatest impact on the selection process. And, because the East-West game encompassed all of the Negro League teams, not just two Negro World Series foes, more of the fans' favorite players would be featured at one time, in one place.

Another key to the game's success and popularity was its central location. Fans, most of whom were black and from the economically depressed South, could not afford to travel great distances to see a World Series game being played in New York City, for example, especially since the dates for the series changed from one year to the next. But fans could count on the East-West game being held at Chicago's Comiskey Park every August. Entire families planned months in advance to see the contest, and the event was turned into what today might be called a "minivacation." People from all over the Midwest and several southern states made the trek.

The East-West All-Star Game, Lester adds, was probably more heavily promoted and certainly given greater media attention than was the Negro League World Series. Indeed, from its inception in 1933 through at least the late 1940s, the East-West clash so electrified all baseball fans that white journalists joined with their black peers in covering the event for their respective newspapers and magazines.

In its early stages the game drew about 20,000 fans. By the time Jackie Robinson was making a splash in organized baseball in 1946 with the Dodgers' Montreal farm club, the Negro Leagues' annual East-West All-Star Game was delighting some 50,000 fans who gladly bought their tickets at big-league prices.

A list of those who competed in East-West All-Star games over the years reads like a *Who's Who* of Negro League baseball: Satchel Paige, Josh Gibson, Ray Dandridge, Buck Leonard, Mule Suttles, Martin Dihigo, Ted Radcliffe, Jimmie Crutchfield, Willie Wells, and "Cool Papa" Bell are just some of the luminaries who starred in the midsummer classic.

"We considered it an honor to be there with all the other great Negro League ballplayers of our day," Radcliffe says. "The people got to see some great baseball. Even the white fans came out to watch the East-West game."

Hall of Fame third baseman Ray Dandridge once roomed with Willie Mays in the New York Giants' farm system.

James "Cool Papa" Bell as he appeared in the uniform of the St. Louis Stars, his first professional club.

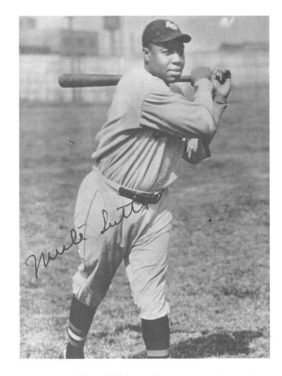

George "Mule" Suttles was a slugging first baseman/outfielder who had a thirty-year career in the Negro Leagues.

Chapter 4:

Road Food And Food For Thought

Throughout the first half of this century, America's two-lane blacktops and dusty dirt roads were the arteries connecting the heart of Negro League baseball with its body of enthusiastic fans.

Bicycles, horse-drawn wagons, trucks, trains, planes, and cars all carried the ballplayers to the towns and cities that supported black baseball, but it was buses—especially the buses—that are most closely associated with travel in the days of the Negro Leagues.

> *Talkin' to myself again*
> *And wonderin' if this travelin' is good*
> *Is there somethin' else a-doin'*
> *We'd be doin' if we could*
> *But ahh, the stories we can tell*
> *And if it all blows up and goes to hell*
> *I can still see us sittin' on a bed in some motel*
> *Listenin' to the stories we can tell*
> **—John Sebastian,** songwriter/performing artist, from his song "Stories We Could Tell"

"When I was younger and playing in the Negro Leagues," says Cuban-born Armando Vazquez, "we journeyed by nothing but old buses. Miles and miles of bus travel. We'd sleep on the bus, eat on the bus, sing on the bus, play cards on the bus. All the time we were on the bus.

"Once in a while, if the bus broke down, we'd have to find cars or, if we were in a city, taxis, to take us to the ballpark in time for the game.

"Sometimes, if we were supposed to get hotel rooms in some town where we were going to play four or five games over a couple of days, we'd say to the club secretary, 'No, you give us that sleepin' money and we'll use it to buy some *real* food.' Baloney sandwiches, apples, cheese, milk, pop, and candy bars were what we usually had, you know, 'cause the white restaurants and roadside cafes wouldn't serve us colored ballplayers."

Vazquez would know. As a naive teenager a thousand miles from his home in Havana, he entered a Nashville restaurant at about midnight following a grueling doubleheader between his team and another all-black squad.

"They threw me out," Vazquez recalls. "They told me, 'You gotta go to the back door to buy what you want. You can't come in here.' I got so mad when they told me that, that I decided not to do what they told me. So when I saw a little guy with a small truck filled with watermelon I went over and bought one watermelon from him.

"I ate the whole thing, I was so hungry. But I got so sick after that, that I couldn't sleep that night. I remember that because it happened so early in my career."

Vazquez's run-in with management at the whites-only eatery was an ugly scene that mirrored similar scenes that had transpired before it and would, sadly, be repeated many

Opposite page: Armando Vazquez was a reliable utility player in the Negro Leagues from 1944 through 1952. He once was part of an infield that included future home-run king Hank Aaron.

times afterward—even to black ballplayers in the integrated major leagues. (Curt Flood, star center fielder for the St. Louis Cardinals in the 1960s, tells of having to eat at "black" restaurants and kicking back at "black" bars after a game—and this was in the late 1950s and early 1960s, years after the majors' color line had been broken.)

Speedy first baseman George Giles, a member of the Negro National League's St. Louis Stars, which captured back-to-back pennants in 1930 and 1931, echoes Vazquez's recollections of life on the road. Giles, who claims he was "never much of a social bug anyway," shied away from situations that were potentially offensive or even dangerous to blacks.

"The racism we faced while I was in the Negro Leagues was one of the things that eventually pushed me out of baseball," Giles says. "I was treated like a second-class citizen in my own country by people who knew they hated me before I could even say 'Hello.'

"Because of that, I didn't socialize much after the game, even with my own teammates, and never with the white ballplayers during a barnstorming tour. I pretty much stayed away from the nightlife. I'd usually go and get some ice cream, or go to a show, before heading back to the hotel or wherever it was where we were staying.

"I kind of went off on my own a lot. I didn't party much, but I was curious about the world. I enjoyed meeting people and learning about things. The travel was hard. Ridin' those buses in those days wasn't the easiest way to get around. But the friendships that formed from bein' on the bus like that kind of made up for it. And baseball, of course. I loved the game.

"And playing baseball in the Negro Leagues gave me a chance to see places and things I'd never seen before. Traveling around the country opened my eyes. Along the way I was meeting and associating with all those different people from all walks of life—doctors, lawyers, teachers, businesspeople. Experience is a wonderful thing, and I was able to pass that on to my family. I could use that as a guideline for my kids, and it turned out all right because all four of 'em graduated from college."

Fatigue and hunger joined caution as the watchwords of Negro Leaguers on the road. Traveling in cramped, noisy, ovenlike buses, players slept sitting up. Sometimes, a team's star player might be afforded a spot on the floor of the bus. There, lying on a blanket or quilt, he could stretch out his

Josh Gibson, who starred at and behind the plate for twenty years, was a legend throughout the United States, Mexico, and the Carribean. He learned a lot about people in his travels and passed that knowledge on to his son, Josh Jr., who also played in the Negro Leagues.

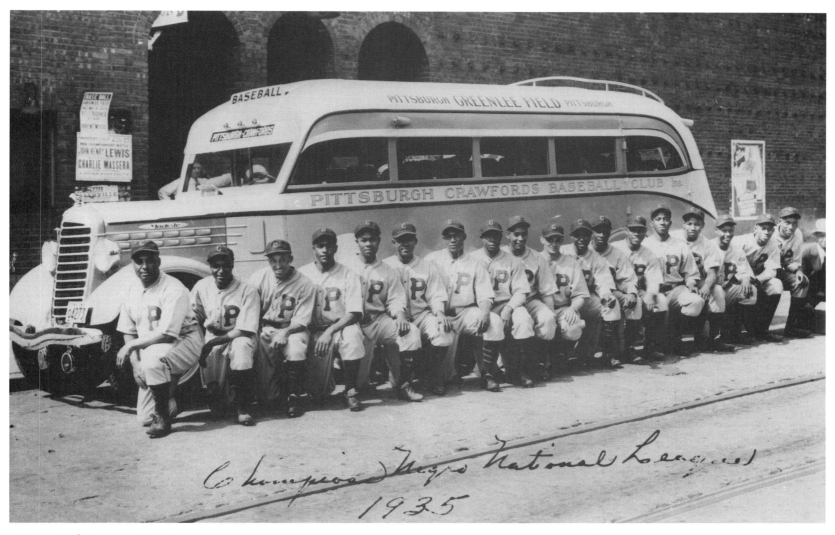

This 1936 photo of the Pittsburgh Crawfords notes the team's World Series win over the New York Cubans the year before.

weary limbs, and woe to any rookie who made the mistake of tripping over a sleeping veteran and waking him up.

Round-trips of hundreds of miles in one day were commonplace. There was little time between scheduled games to enjoy a relaxing, hot, sit-down meal at establishments that catered to blacks, so on the way the teams made pit stops at mom-and-pop stores or roadside stands to stock up on loaves of bread, lunch meat, milk, apples, candy bars, and other items to keep them going until they arrived at their destina-

tion. It was common for the players to live off bologna sandwiches for days at a time.

Negro Leaguers called it a "Dutch lunch," recalls Josh Gibson, Jr., whose brief career in the Negro Leagues and Class-C ball in the minors began about the time his famous father's career ended in the late 1940s. Negro League ballplayers and their coaches survived on such fare, and though the road-weary travelers tired of eating them, those sandwiches kept the men alive.

Not Who's on First, But Who's *in* First?

Throughout its fabled life, black professional baseball was hampered by scheduling problems rooted in the sometimes precarious financial state of the various leagues and their ballclubs. Rained-out games were not always made up at a later date, team owners scheduled money-making exhibition games against nonleague clubs, it was often difficult to guarantee the use of mostly white-owned stadiums. These are only a few examples of the factors that helped to undermine efforts to standardize league schedules. According to several players interviewed for this book, the won-lost records of two teams in the same league at season's end might show a difference in the total number of games played of as many as ten, fifteen, or even twenty. It's little wonder that pennant races, the World Series, and playoff games failed to mean as much to the fans as the annual East-West All-Star Game.

Above: Managers Frank Duncan (left) and Raleigh "Biz" Mackey in the 1940s. Below: The East won the 1937 All-Star Game 7–2.

As a boy growing up in Pittsburgh, home base for legendary Negro League clubs the Crawfords and the Homestead Grays, Josh Jr. was cautioned by his father: "Read the signs. You'll see 'colored' and 'whites only' in your travels, son, especially in the South. Don't try anything foolish."

He generally paid heed to his father's words. But one of the teams for which Josh Jr. played featured a player who could pass for white.

"Oh, we used to send him into places that were for whites only, all right," Gibson recalls with a laugh, "and he'd buy hot food and cold drinks for us while we sat out in the bus, out of sight from everybody else. Except for the restaurants, hotels, and private homes where black ballplayers could eat and rest up, it was the only way for us to get something besides sandwiches. Just like with the style of play in the Negro Leagues, we had to be creative to survive."

Team officials anxious to keep their operations afloat often scheduled multiple contests in different communities on the same day. This taxed the players' stamina and patience further.

"Hey, I can remember that sometimes we'd play *three* games in one day, like the Fourth of July," insists Armando Vazquez. "The first game would start at ten o'clock in the morning, the second one at two o'clock in the afternoon, and the third one early in the evening—sometimes in three different towns. We'd be so tired that night that we could hardly walk. But then we'd get on the bus and travel to the next town to play a doubleheader the next day. I think that's why we sang on the bus: to keep our spirits up. Man, you *had* to love the game to do what we did back then, 'cause we *sure* didn't do it for the money."

Whenever the team bus or automobile broke down the players and their coaches assumed the role of auto mechanics. Former Negro Leaguers now pepper their remembrances with damning praise for the rickety old buses that carried them from one diamond to the next.

Sometimes, the bus never completed the journey. One harrowing experience in the early 1950s began innocently enough after the Kansas City Monarchs left a spring training site in Jacksonville, Florida, for their next stop in Miami. Players and coaches were sound asleep in the early morning hours as their bus driver took them south along a darkened stretch of Highway A1A.

Throughout the 1940s, Mahlon Duckett was a top-notch infielder with the Philadelphia Stars and the Homestead Grays.

Bucking the Trend

John "Buck" O'Neil, former first baseman and manager of the Kansas City Monarchs, was named Major League Baseball's first black coach. It happened in 1962 with the Chicago Cubs. O'Neil had served as a scout for the team for six years prior to donning Cubs pinstripes.

Part of K.C.'s brain trust: manager Buck O'Neil (left) and travel secretary William "Dizzy" Dismukes, himself a former player and manager in the Negro Leagues.

An interior storage compartment located at the rear of the bus, over the engine, was filled with the team's equipment and a few personal belongings. Something—a few eyewitnesses say it was shoe polish rags—started smoldering in the storage compartment, which was becoming hotter by the minute from the heat of the engine.

The driver stopped the bus and got out to determine the cause of the smoke. When he opened the engine cover, air was sucked into the storage compartment and quickened the combustion process. Flames shot up and all aboard scurried out of the old bus. No one was injured, but the Monarchs lost nearly all of their belongings, including bats, gloves, uniforms, and shoes. The bus was a total loss.

It was some time before a passing motorist finally came by and picked up the team's traveling secretary and Buck O'Neil, the Monarchs' manager, and drove them to a phone, where they called team owner Tom Baird. Baird then called a bus company in Miami and arranged for another bus to pick up his stranded team. The Monarchs were at the fire scene for several hours before they were rescued, but they arrived in Miami later that day in time to play their next opponent—in borrowed uniforms and ill-fitting spikes, and using unfamiliar gloves and bats.

Another story comes from the annals of the Memphis Red Sox. The team was late departing its home base for a game in nearby Clarksdale, Mississippi, and the bus driver lead-footed it down Highway 61.

They weren't on the road for more than an hour or two when they heard the highway patrol car's siren wailing behind them. Homer "Goose" Curry, an outfielder/pitcher-turned-manager, shot to the back of the bus, sprawled across a seat and pretended to be asleep as the bus driver braked to a stop.

"Hey, boy! Didn't you know you was speedin' out here?!" the patrolman barked at the bus driver.

"I'm sorry, sir, I guess I didn't know I was goin' so fast."

"Well, I'm gonna hafta write you up a ticket. You know that, don't you?"

Just then, Curry "awakened" from his slumbers and staggered to the front of the bus, where he poked his head out the driver's window.

"Officer, officer, officer. What's the problem here? My name's Homer Curry. I'm the manager of this ball club. Can I help?"

"Your driver was speedin' and I'm gonna cite him for breakin' the law," came the terse reply.

Curry, still feigning grogginess, looked at his driver and snapped, "I *told* you not to be speeding on this highway! You get off this bus right *now*. You're fired!"

Monarchs owner J. L. Wilkinson (second from left) stands with members of his team and some House of David players, circa 1934. Wilkinson was an innovator and was instrumental in bringing night games to all of professional baseball.

The patrolman seemed surprised. "Well, now, I wouldn't be too hard on him."

"Yeah, well, I don't want him no more. He disobeyed my order not to speed on this highway." Curry looked at the driver and repeated his demand: "Get off this bus right now, you hear me?"

As the driver stood up to grab his coat and travel bag, the patrolman said, "No, no! Don't make him get off the bus clear out here. I tell you what. I won't write him a ticket if you let him keep his job."

Curry looked at his driver, then at the patrolman, and said, "Well, all right, officer. I thank you. And I'll make sure he doesn't do it again." And with that, the patrolman smiled and stepped away from the bus, visibly pleased with himself for his magnanimous gesture toward a poor, colored bus driver.

As the driver slowly steered the bus back onto the highway, Curry heaved a sigh of relief and said, "That was a close one!" and the entire bus rocked with laughter.

On the downside of millions of miles of road travel were the more serious vehicular accidents. Fortunately, they were few and far between. Considering the long hours Negro Leaguers spent on the road, it's surprising that tragedy didn't strike more often. One such incident resulted in outfielder "Wild Bill" Wright gaining more playing time at the expense of a teammate.

Wright tells of the time when his club was on its way to play a game in Toledo, Ohio. The driver of the car in which the players were riding attempted to pass a truck on a long, lonely stretch of highway, but in the process apparently pulled the car much too close to the truck.

According to Wright, the team's center fielder was leaning out of the car too far, perhaps gesturing with his arm to illustrate a point, "and his arm was torn right off," Wright says.

"It was bad. He was forced to quit baseball, and I became the team's regular center fielder. I wanted to get more playing time, but not that way. All of us felt terrible that such a thing could happen."

There are some who would say that familiarity breeds contempt, but infighting among teammates in the Negro Leagues was less frequent than one might think, considering the sardinelike existence these wandering ballplayers led for so many years. Surviving players now emphasize that when they were on the road, away from their homes and chummier surroundings, they had few people to turn to except each other. Jim Crow, not one's teammates, was the enemy. So, while no club was free of arguments, shoving matches, or snubs of rookies by veterans, it's important to remember another adage when pondering life in the Negro Leagues: there is safety in numbers.

Opposite page: Second baseman Newton "Newt" Allen (seated at far left) and pitching star Wilbur "Bullet" Rogan (seated, center) once proudly wore the Monarchs jersey. Fans identified with team logos and pennants then just as they do today.

KANSAS CITY MONARCH
WORLDS COLORED CHAMPIONS
BASE BALL CLUB

Catcher Josh Gibson and runner Henry Milton collide in the 1939 East-West All-Star Game, which Milton's West squad won 4–2.

Nonetheless, incidents and conflicts of various kinds did occur, both off the field and on it. Some of these confrontations involved teammates; others involved players from rival franchises.

And of course, what organized league would be complete without the tradition of heaping abuse on the umpires? Players charged umps after close calls at the plate or on the bases. Fans fired bottles at the umps because they blamed the officials for the home team's bitter defeat. Managers and coaches were sent to the showers early, courtesy of an umpire who disliked that last remark made about his parentage. And on at least one occasion an umpire found all four of his car tires slashed—perhaps a fan's way of saying "thanks" for calling a great game.

Perhaps the scariest moment any umpire in the Negro Leagues ever faced involved Bob Motley. Motley is remembered as one of the fairest arbiters in the leagues' history, a man who understood the rule book as well as he understood human nature, and in the process earned the respect of nearly all who met him.

As was the custom of the period, one umpire was assigned to ride with a given team, to save on travel expenses. A game between the Monarchs and another club ended when a young Motley, who would go on to be named umpire in chief of the Negro American League and who later officiated at organized baseball's Triple-A level in the Pacific Coast League for nearly eight seasons, called the opposing runner "safe" on a close play at the plate.

That night on the Monarchs' bus, miles outside of town along a desolate stretch of road, one of the Kansas City players turned around in his seat and accused Motley of blowing the call and costing the Monarchs the game. Motley tried to ignore the insults. The player suddenly brandished a hunting knife and walked toward the wide-eyed Motley seated at the back of the bus.

"I'm gonna cut your black ass," the player bellowed. But when the player reached manager Buck O'Neil's seat, O'Neil jumped up, stood nose-to-nose with the hothead, and growled:

"You touch that umpire and you will never play another ballgame as long as you live. So you siddown, boy, you hear me?"

But life on the road also gave rise to more amusing anecdotes that enrich the oral and written histories of life in the Negro Leagues. And while the smooth and sometimes sardonic Satchel Paige was generally considered the Negro Leagues' resident wit during his lifetime, even the friendly but businesslike Josh Gibson was no stranger to dry humor. Josh Gibson, Jr., recalls an exchange that took place when he was batboy for his father's team, the Homestead Grays, some fifty years ago:

Future Hall-of-Famer Josh Gibson at bat in a 1945 midsummer contest at Washington's Griffith Stadium.

Sr.: If I ever get beaned and am out cold on the ground, run to be the first one at my side.

Jr.: To see if you're all right?

Sr.: No, because I want you to take my billfold out of my back pocket before anybody else gets there.

The quick-thinking Goose Curry of the fabled Mississippi speeding ticket incident didn't have his billfold lifted when he played for the Philadelphia Stars. He had himself lifted—onto a stretcher.

Curry, the Stars' talented right fielder, ran in quickly on a line drive hit off the bat of the Monarchs' first baseman, Buck O'Neil. Curry lost the ball in the sun, however, and it thudded off his forehead. A teammate backing him up on the play grabbed the ball and fired it into the infield as O'Neil slid into second.

Time was called. Players and coaches from both teams ran to the fallen Curry.

"You all right, Goose?"

"Yeah, I'm all right. I'm feeling pretty good, I guess."

"Look, we're gonna help you to your feet and if you can walk you can leave the game to have that bump on your head looked at."

"*No!*" Curry protested to the circle of concerned faces. "I don't want to walk by all these people in this ballpark after I let a ball hit me between the eyes. What you do is, you put me on a stretcher and carry me outta here, past everybody, OK?"

The men obliged Goose, and as he was carried away on the stretcher, the fans gave him a standing ovation for his efforts. Curry, milking the situation for all it was worth, waved weakly to the crowd.

From the late 1940s until the Negro Leagues' final gasps in the early 1960s, "war stories" were not limited to baseball patter. The men of the Negro Leagues traded actual war stories from their days in uniform, serving their country in World War II or the Korean War.

Once Jackie Robinson shattered baseball's color line in 1947 and other black ballplayers slowly but surely gained admittance to the big leagues, attendance began dropping at Negro League games. However, this May 1953 contest at Kansas City drew more than 18,000 fans.

Some, like future umpire Bob Motley, saw action. Motley was stationed in Saipan in the mid-1940s when he was wounded in the foot by a sniper's bullet. Bob and a fellow soldier had just finished digging their foxhole, and Motley propped his feet up on the lip of the foxhole to take a nap. Had he exposed his head and not his feet, Motley says, still cringing at the thought, "I'd be in another world right now."

Another, Bob Thurman, was a first sergeant in the infantry stationed in New Guinea when he faced a deadly enemy of a different kind. Sleeping in his tent at about 2 A.M., Thurman was awakened by the sounds of a large, growling animal pawing at the canvas. Thurman unholstered his .45 automatic pistol and, sensing the creature was about to claw its way through the fabric, fired shot after shot into the outstretched silhouette. Thurman's men rushed over to find their sergeant had "bagged a lion."

The effervescent Paige, though, remains the most frequently tapped source of wisdom and one-liners of the Negro Leagues. Even while he was alive, Satchel's exploits on the diamond, and his witticisms off it, were legendary. He is credited with having admonished teammates and acquaintances alike to "Avoid fried meats, which angry up the blood," and, "Keep the juices flowing by jangling around gently as you move." One of his more famous maxims, "Go very light on the vices, such as carrying on in society—the society ramble ain't restful," was particularly amusing when one considers the busy social calendar Satchel had as a young man.

Indeed, after-hours entertainment for the Negro Leaguers encompassed all of the usual trappings associated with the white major leagues. Baseball Annies (that is, single women attracted to ballplayers) were as commonplace in the Negro Leagues at that time as they were in the majors. It was not unusual for Negro Leaguers, single or married, to have girlfriends in the cities that hosted black professional baseball.

Particularly in bustling metropolitan areas with large black populations such as New York, Kansas City, Chicago, St. Louis, and Pittsburgh, players were exposed to the speakeasies, nightclubs, and fancy restaurants that spotlighted Count Basie, Louis Armstrong, Cab Calloway, Eubie Blake, Bill "Mr. Bojangles" Robinson, and other legendary black performers of the 1920s, 1930s, and 1940s.

Opposite page: Singing legend Ella Fitzgerald (seated at left) is joined by an all-star group of major league ballplayers that included Don Newcombe (second man in on the left) and Larry Doby (next to "Newk"). The first four gentlemen across from Ella are (from end) Joe Black, Connie Johnson, Junior Gilliam, and Bob Boyd.

The Roaring Twenties witnessed "Cool Papa" Bell's professional baseball debut in 1922 and the Negro Leagues' first World Series in 1924.

Color It Exciting

Black professional baseball held its first postseason crown jewel, the Negro League World Series, in 1924. The match-up involved the Hilldale Giants and the Kansas City Monarchs. To generate fan interest beyond that found in the two host cities and allow as many people as possible to see the top two black teams "go at it," organizers arranged to hold the Series in several cities where Negro League baseball flourished. So, in addition to Philadelphia and Kansas City, games were played in Chicago and Baltimore. The Monarchs edged the Giants, 5 games to 4, with one tie, to win the first Negro League World Series. Several of the games were won by one run.

Negro Leaguers still living in the Midwest fondly recall such venues as Fox's Tavern, the El Capitan Club, the Orpheum, and the Eblon Theater, where jazz and the blues were part of Kansas City's heady late-night mix, which rivaled that of the hot spots in the Big Apple and Windy City.

"Kansas City was an exchange point for many travel arteries," explains Negro Leagues researcher Larry Lester. "In 1915, many southern blacks who migrated to northern cities—for example, to Chicago—never made it to their intended destinations. They wound up staying in Kansas City."

Black entertainers, like black ballplayers and black people in general, were drawn to Kansas City, the halfway point between New York City and Los Angeles. Big-name entertainers based in New York would also get top dollar to play for audiences out on the West Coast, but they soon discovered that with so many blacks living in Kansas City it was well worth their time to schedule gigs there during their cross-country train trips.

Black players weren't immune to the fast life—jazz and blues, women, gambling—outside the realm of baseball. It was all there for the taking. But to the players, the game itself remained of paramount importance.

As George Giles, who generally shunned the night life and its pitfalls, says: "Even those guys who did go out and party took their baseball seriously when the game was being played. No one wanted to embarrass himself out there on the field. We played hard. We cared about the game, and we took pride in the fact that we were professional ballplayers."

Adds Armando Vazquez, "Okay, so we didn't make much money, we traveled a lot in old buses, and some places wouldn't serve us. But we were playin' baseball, man, and we had a lot of fun doing it."

Away from the ballpark: Clifford "Connie" Johnson, Joe Black, and Jim "Junior" Gilliam—all of whom later starred in the majors—relax with their dates at a popular nightspot (opposite page). Representatives of the Pittsburgh Crawfords from the 1930s stand proudly next to their team bus (above).

Chapter 5:

Bordering On Greatness

Typically earning low wages and facing racial prejudice in the United States nearly every day of their lives drove many of the Negro Leaguers south of the border to play professionally.

Throughout Mexico, Cuba, the Dominican Republic, Puerto Rico, Panama, and neighboring countries, waves of Negro League stars were welcomed with open arms and very often with open checkbooks.

Satchel Paige, Josh Gibson, Chet Brewer, Willie Wells, Ray Dandridge, Bill Wright, Leon Day, Monte Irvin, Roy Campanella, and dozens of other top-notch ballplayers in the Negro Leagues forged parallel careers in those warm climes.

Many black players learned Spanish as a second language. Some developed managerial skills that served them well on both sides of the border. The big-name Negro Leaguers pulled in substantial salaries for that time, but even the utility players could make a nice chunk of change by playing for the rich and powerful Latin American club owners who enticed them to come south of the border.

The Negro Leaguers' aggressive style of play had a marked influence on pro ball throughout Latin America. While tape-measure home runs were always a welcome sight to any crowd, taking the extra base, the bunt-and-run, the hit-and-run, and other plays—if successfully executed—thrilled the fans even more. Black ballplayers earned a great deal of respect and admiration for their smarts as well as their skills.

> *Every night when I go to bed I pray to the Lord and thank him for giving me the ability to play ball.*
> —**Roy Campanella,** Hall of Fame catcher for the Brooklyn Dodgers and a former star with the Baltimore Elite Giants

Most important to the Negro Leaguers, perhaps, was that in the Latin American nations they were accepted as men possessing rights equal to those of other men. For these black ballplayers, the United States was their homeland but south of the border was where many of them rediscovered their self-worth as human beings.

A few players, disgusted with their treatment as second-class citizens in Jim Crow America, eventually chose to remain in their adopted countries. Others simply made it a habit to divide their time between the Negro Leagues and the Latin American leagues.

Josh Gibson, Jr., says that he really didn't get to know his famous father very well until just before the latter's death in January of 1947. "That's because he was always in Cuba or Mexico when he wasn't playing for the Grays back in Pittsburgh.

Opposite page: Newark Eagles mound ace Leon Day as he appeared in 1943.

"He was well liked by the fans and the team owners down there. He was very popular. He would tell me how he was treated with respect by the people there. I know he enjoyed playing in those other countries. He had a lot of stories to tell us about his trips down there. He had fun. He liked it down there."

Josh Jr. recounts how his father, despite long absences from the Gibson family home in Pittsburgh, was still keenly interested in the lives of his children, who were raised by a grandmother after the children's mother died when they were babies. One story in particular serves to illustrate that point.

"My father would keep tabs on us kids to make sure we were doing our lessons and staying out of trouble," Josh Jr. begins, laughing with a smoker's hack. "The way he would do that was to come back at certain times of the year and ask my grandmother. She told him *everything*.

"I was about fifteen at the time. Months before he came home, I had used a cussword at my sister. My father came home from playin' ball in the Latin countries and oh, man,

my grandmother had waited *all winter long* to tell him what I'd done. He took one of his alligator belts and hit me just one time across my back. That's all it took for me to behave myself from then on. I got one whippin' from my father, and that was it."

Josh Gibson, Sr., wasn't the only famous Negro Leaguer to attain superstar status playing baseball in Latin America.

Ray Dandridge, the legendary Negro League third baseman who was inducted into the National Baseball Hall of Fame in 1987, tore up the leagues south of the border. The "dandy one" batted .350 or better year after year for several teams in Mexico and Cuba. He topped the .370 mark in 1948 and was crowned the Mexican League batting champ. Monte Irvin and Roy Campanella are two other former Negro League greats who enjoyed success in Latin America. They, too, are enshrined in the Hall of Fame at Cooperstown.

For a dozen years, Bill Wright was a superb contact hitter and fleet outfielder for the Baltimore Elite Giants and several other Negro League teams. In the mid-1940s, having already enjoyed success in professional leagues outside the United States, Wright made his home in Mexico. When a reunion of former Negro Leaguers was held in Chicago in 1991, Wright made the 1,500-mile trip by plane and bus to be there. It was only the second time in forty years he had been in the United States.

There is a matter-of-factness in his voice when Bill Wright talks of his life in baseball as player, coach, and manager—particularly of the times after he decided to live and work outside the United States. "Wild Bill," so named after a brief stint early in his career as a pitcher with control problems, says:

"I tell you true. I liked everything about playing baseball. I could hit. I could run. I could throw with accuracy. I always tried to help the team. And later on, I enjoyed managing,

Josh Gibson, Jr. (opposite page) followed in his dad's footsteps as a professional baseball player. A life-threatening kidney ailment curtailed Junior's career, but his enjoyment of the game hasn't diminished with age. He maintains a wonderful photo album of Josh Sr.'s life on and off the field, and notes with great pride that his dad had a great sense of humor to go with his celebrated prowess as a ballplayer. In his youth, Junior served as a batboy for the Homestead Grays, one of two Pittsburgh-based teams for which his dad starred as catcher (the Crawfords were the other). Junior may have witnessed this close play (above) involving his hard-charging dad and catcher Ted "Double Duty" Radcliffe.

enjoyed teaching the younger ballplayers how to play the game, how to do the little things to win ballgames, how to hit to all fields.

"But I remember a time here in the States in the 1930s when a handpicked all-star team of guys from the Elites, the team I played for, and guys from clubs like the Crawfords and the Grays in Pittsburgh, played a doubleheader against an all-white team managed by Rogers Hornsby.

"We beat them in both games of that doubleheader. The next day, the newspaper came out and said the Rogers Hornsby All-Stars showed the fans how baseball should be played. The paper didn't say nothin' about us beatin' 'em in a doubleheader. That's the kind of prejudice the colored ballplayers faced back then. We had a hard time convincing people we were for real.

"A lot of people today think we were just standin' around out there on the ballfield in our baseball uniforms and spikes, that we couldn't do anything, or that we clowned around. But we played good baseball in the Negro Leagues, and we showed the major league players we were as good as—and in

In Cuba, from left to right: Terris McDuffie, an unknown player, catcher Quincy Trouppe, Lenny Pearson, another unknown player, Willie Mays, Joe Black, and Ray Dandridge.

some cases, better than—they were. But, I still feel I was one of the luckiest guys in baseball, I suppose. I even put myself into a game when I was seventy-one years old and slapped a couple of hits. Couldn't run, though."

Many Negro Leaguers playing south of the United States–Mexico border benefited not only from better salaries, but from enhanced status, too. Wright notes that he was one of dozens of "good, solid ballplayers" who did well in the Negro Leagues in the United States but who truly flourished in Mexico and Latin America because of the greater freedom blacks enjoyed in those countries.

The Double-A Minneapolis Millers' Ray Dandridge (left, running) spent most of his professional career in the Negro Leagues. He never got the call to the "bigs," but his accomplishments as a player (and later as a manager) were so well known that they propelled him into the Hall of Fame. Another Negro Leagues star who went on to manage was shortstop Willie Wells (above).

A Decade of Screwballs

Verdell Mathis was a bright, determined young man of eighteen when he embarked on a professional baseball career in 1940. His demeanor, however, was in sharp contrast to the name for his "out" pitch: the screwball. So good was he at getting this pitch past opposing batters—particularly righthanded batters—that "Lefty" was often called on to pitch for his team in the bigger games (and against opposing teams' own aces). He won back-to-back East-West All-Star games in 1944 and 1945. Mathis played his entire career with the Memphis Red Sox.

To underscore the irony of the situation, blacks and whites found themselves in the same uniforms when millionaire club owners such as Jorge Pasquel lured a number of major league players to jump the National and American leagues and play full-time for the highly competitive teams in Mexico, Cuba, and other Caribbean nations.

Catcher Mickey Owen and pitchers Sal "the Barber" Maglie and Max Lanier were among the white big leaguers who

headed south for a few seasons in the late 1940s. Most of Lanier's memories of those years, when blacks, whites, and Hispanics were teammates, remain positive. He notes that players, regardless of their color, were sometimes offered side money by owners and fans alike if the players performed certain feats, such as winning a hotly contested pitching duel against a hated rival or slugging a home run with the bases loaded.

In other instances, people would place bets on what a given player would or would not do during the course of a game. This was particularly prevalent in Mexico, according to Bob Thurman. He recalls an incident in winter involving his friend and teammate from the Homestead Grays, Josh Gibson.

It seems the great catcher failed to hit a home run in a game and there had been numerous bets placed on him to do so. After the game, Josh and a few other players walked to one of their favorite watering holes for drinks. The bartender, apparently out "mucho dinero" because of Gibson, avenged his gambling loss by slipping the catcher a Mickey Finn. Josh's evening was soon over.

Lanier emphasizes that the caliber of play in the Latin American leagues was very strong. How could it be otherwise? With some big names from the majors and the cream of the Negro Leagues teaming up with the top Hispanic ballplayers, it could well be argued that the best, most exciting baseball of the day was being played outside the United States.

Josh Gibson (opposite page, right) was a national hero in Cuba, one of several countries in which Negro Leaguers had for years enjoyed personal as well as professional satisfaction. Many teams were integrated, and all ballplayers were free to associate with one another in society. The Almendares Blues Baseball Club of 1947 (above) included St. Louis Cardinals hurler Max Lanier (seated, second from left).

In Mexico, Cuba, and the other Latin American countries, the only "race" issue that cropped up came whenever a runner and an opposing fielder raced each other to the bag on a close play.

Winning was still the name of the game. Blacks, whites, and Hispanics functioned as equals between the foul lines, in the dugout and the locker room, and on the bus. They were able to eat in the same restaurants and stay at the same hotels.

On the field, players accepted the coaching, cajoling, tips, and good-natured ribbing from their teammates no matter what their color. Nineteenth-century pitching ace Tony Mullane, who ignored the signals from black battery mate Fleet Walker, would have been sent packing if he'd behaved in his usual way as part of any racially integrated Latin team. And the notorious Cap Anson? With his attitude he never would have been allowed to suit up and take the field. His white teammates would have seen to that.

Miles away—both literally and figuratively—from the United States' shameful social barriers, blacks and whites interacted more freely with one another off as well as on the field. The white players' admiration and respect for the Negro Leaguers and their innovative style of play grew, and not a few genuine friendships developed. Integration, then, was doing just fine beyond U.S. borders.

The 1945 American All-Stars, based in Caracas, Venezuela, included such Negro League luminaries as Jackie Robinson (kneeling, at left), Gene Benson (next to Robinson), Sam Jethroe (kneeling, next to the trainer), Roy Campanella (standing, second from left), Quincy Trouppe (standing, center), and Buck Leonard (standing, far right).

"The Apollo of the Box," as Tony Mullane was dubbed by some, won 30 or more games over five consecutive seasons in the 1880s when the distance from the pitching rubber to home plate was only fifty feet. The one person he had trouble pitching to was his catcher, a black man named Fleet Walker. Mullane disliked men of color, and usually ignored the signals from his battery mate behind the plate.

Even in Canada, black players often found greater freedom and respect than they did in the United States, the so-called land of the free.

"You were a ballplayer and that was it," says Josh Gibson, Jr., of his baseball tours of duty in Canada. "We went to a white barber. We ate at integrated restaurants with no incident. And, if you had to go to the bathroom and you wound up standing in line behind a white man and in front of a white woman, there was no problem, no prejudice.

"The only prejudice we saw was when we would come to the New York state line, where Americans would react differently to us black ballplayers."

Even George Giles, who concentrated his professional baseball career in the United States, reflects on the sentiment, shared by many, that there was no earthly reason for blacks and whites in the States to play the game in separate worlds, and for integration of the major leagues to be so long in coming.

"People say to me, 'George, you were born too soon to be one of the ones to make it to the big leagues.' But I didn't have nothin' to do with that.

"And besides, I was born in the United States of America. I'm an *American*, not a foreigner. For years, foreigners came here and had more opportunity than I had. It didn't seem right, but that was the American way of life. Blacks got along okay with white and Latin players down south, so why couldn't it work out up here? Yes, I guess I was surprised when Jackie got the call. I never thought it was goin' to happen. Never thought they'd let us in.

"I mean, blacks and whites are playin' together now and there's no problem, is there? They're playin' baseball, football, basketball together *now*. How come they couldn't do it back then? What was wrong with *us*? Why'd they wait so long to bring black ballplayers to the big leagues?"

Chapter 6:

After The War, Another Battlefront

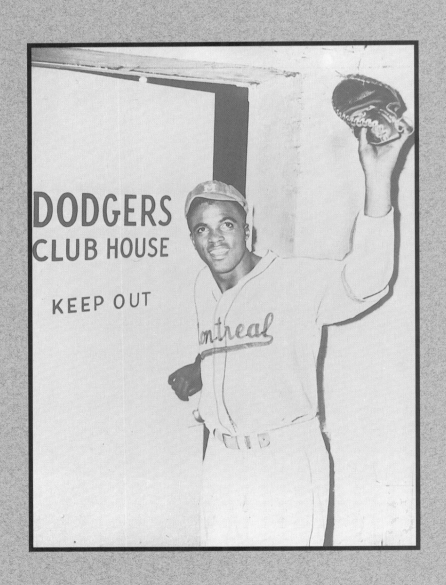

P erhaps the supreme irony of the Negro Leagues is that the decade that witnessed their greatest following also spurred their lingering demise.

For the leagues' participants and spectators alike, there was little reason to think the 1940s would be any different from preceding years. Organized baseball was still lily white. Black players were still denied the opportunity to compete against the country's top white players except for postseason barnstorming tours. Commissioner Kenesaw Mountain Landis still clandestinely blocked any effort by big-league owners to integrate organized baseball. Black people in general were still denied access to many restaurants, hotels, schools, parks, and other establishments across the United States, which put Jim Crow customs and laws ahead of a person's fundamental civil rights. It was, in the most tiresome and unenlightened sense of the phrase, "business as usual."

Then the United States' entry into World War II necessitated a crucial rethinking of the country's race relations. As more and more black men fought and died to free oppressed peoples overseas, Americans back home increasingly came to understand the shame of segregation.

For Major League Baseball, that meant dealing with growing pressure to tear down the unwritten color barrier that had been in effect for nearly sixty years. People reasoned that if a black man can risk injury and death in the service of his country, why can't he play baseball in the majors? Or, as some ardent integrationists demanded, If this is the land of opportunity, prove it.

If a black boy can make it on Okinawa and Guadalcanal, hell, he can make it in baseball.
—Baseball Commissioner A. B. "Happy" Chandler in 1945, answering a black reporter's question about integrating the game.

Several feeble attempts—some sincere, others not—to ease blacks into organized white baseball occurred periodically during the war years.

In 1942, Jack Roosevelt Robinson, an All-America running back for the UCLA Bruins and a multisports star for the school, and Nate Moreland, a talented pitcher with the Baltimore Elite Giants and the Kansas City Monarchs in the Negro Leagues (who later pitched in Class-C organized baseball on the West Coast), were granted a tryout with the Chicago White Sox at the club's Southern California training facilities. Skipper Jimmy Dykes later spoke glowingly of Robinson in particular, but failed to push club ownership to do anything further with either of the men.

Opposite page: This photograph of Jackie Robinson, taken in spring of 1947, is worth much more than a thousand words.

In 1943, Washington Senators owner Clark Griffith, a teammate of the infamous baseball bigot Cap Anson during the 1890s, met with Negro League superstars Josh Gibson and Buck Leonard. "The Old Fox," as he was called, discussed the possibility of their playing in the big leagues. Although both Gibson and Leonard were enthusiastic about the idea of playing in the majors, Griffith never followed up on the matter, and the pair returned to Pittsburgh and resumed play for the Homestead Grays.

That same year, Pittsburgh Pirates owner William Benswanger first scheduled, then canceled, a tryout for Dave Barnhill, a pitcher for the New York Cubans, and Roy Campanella, a catcher for the Baltimore Elite Giants. The tryout was to have taken place at the Pirates' home ballpark, Forbes Field, in early August. No satisfactory answer for the cancellation was ever given.

Meanwhile, Bill Veeck, Jr., about to finalize his purchase of the hapless Philadelphia Phillies, was scheming to add several top Negro Leaguers—sluggers, pitchers, and base thieves—to the team's otherwise anemic roster and, in a nearly literal sense, run away with the 1944 National League Championship. The meddling Kenesaw Mountain Landis, however, undermined not only the budding entrepreneur's plan to add black ballplayers to the Phillies, but his effort to buy the

Roy Campanella goes opposite field (above). Had Baseball Commissioner Landis lived to see the integration of Major League Baseball, this likely would have been his reaction (opposite page).

Satchel Paige was well into his forties when he began pitching in the American League. He played for the St. Louis Browns, Cleveland Indians, and Kansas City Athletics.

Phillies in the first place. He accomplished this by informing National League president Ford Frick of Veeck's blueprint for winning.

When Veeck tried to finalize his purchase of the Phillies, he was informed by Frick, who by this time was overseeing the sale of the club, that Frick had personally okayed its sale to businessman William D. Cox for about half of what Veeck was going to fork over. (A final twist to the whole episode is that the following year Landis banished Cox from the game for allegedly betting on his own team.)

In his autobiography, *Veeck—As In Wreck*, the author states: "With Satchel Paige, Roy Campanella, Luke Easter, Monte Irvin, and countless others in action and available, I had not the slightest doubt that in 1944, a war year, the Phils would have leaped from seventh place to the pennant."

Attempts were made to integrate organized baseball at the minor league level that year, too. Nate Moreland, who the year before had joined Jackie Robinson at the White Sox "tryout," didn't even get that far when he and two other Negro Leaguers, infielder Howard Esterling and pitcher Chet Brewer, were informed that their promised tryout with the Los Angeles Angels of the Pacific Coast League had been canceled. Several club owners had pressured the Angels into withdrawing the offer.

Brewer's hopes were dashed again when Oakland Oaks manager Johnny Vergez refused to give Brewer and another black player a tryout, even though owner Vince DeVicenzi had directed Vergez to do so. (Brewer, as knowledgeable as he was talented, eventually managed in the minors after his playing career was over and is remembered today as one of the truly great "finds" of black baseball that the majors missed out on because of the era's prevailing racial attitudes. He won 30 or more games in three consecutive years in the Negro Leagues, but few people today are aware of his feat.)

As one door of opportunity after another was being slammed in their faces, black players continued to ply their trade in the Negro Leagues. Attendance at, and interest in, Negro League games was never better. Not only were regular-season contests faring well at the gate—attracting whites as well as blacks—but during the mid-1940s the Negro Leagues' annual East-West All-Star Game outdrew its all-white equivalent by 20,000 fans or more.

Newt Allen, Monte Irvin, Ted "Double Duty" Radcliffe, Jimmie Crutchfield, Josh Gibson, Dan Bankhead, Leroy "Satchel" Paige, Ray "Hooks" Dandridge, Verdel Mathis, "Wild Bill" Wright, Sam Jethroe, Roy Campanella, Quincy Trouppe, Sam Bankhead, Hilton Smith, and even James "Cool Papa" Bell were among the celebrated Negro Leaguers delighting baseball fans, black and white, in the 1940s.

Whereas the so-called "lively ball" era of the 1920s and 1930s lulled major league fans, coaches, and players into waiting for the home run and the big inning, black professional baseball of that era encouraged what has come to be called "tricky baseball." Tricky baseball included creative ways of manufacturing runs through base stealing, the bunt-and-run, the run-and-hit, special do-or-die sacrifice plays, and other exciting capers.

Fans didn't necessarily want to see white baseball or black baseball, but the best baseball, the most entertaining baseball. It just so happened they found it in the Negro Leagues.

But a vocal few kept pounding away at the hypocrisy of the baseball establishment. Reporters, chiefly black reporters writing in the country's black newspapers and magazines, and several of their sympathetic white peers as well, helped fan the flames of integration and keep the race issue before the public eye.

Privately, some politicians and even a few high-profile persons in organized baseball supported these efforts to integrate the game, but their muted blessings did little to advance the cause.

Frustration over the issue continued to mount for those advocating an about-face in baseball's signing policies regarding blacks. Baseball was dragging its feet.

But on November 25, 1944, a chief hindrance to integration dropped dead of a heart attack in the same city where Andrew

Manager Frank Duncan guided the West squad to a 5–2 victory in the 1947 East-West All-Star Game at Comiskey Park.

Elija "Pumpsie" Green was the first black player to debut with the Boston Red Sox, the last big-league club to integrate.

"Rube" Foster, the Father of Black Baseball, once operated his Chicago American Giants while nurturing his Negro National League.

Kenesaw Mountain Landis, U.S. district court judge turned commissioner of baseball, was gone at the age of seventy-eight. His twenty-four-year reign of absolute power was over. This left an administrative void that proved serendipitous for those advocating integration of the national pastime. Five months after Landis' death, Albert B. Chandler, nicknamed "Happy," was voted Major League Baseball's new commissioner in a runoff election held by the sixteen club owners.

The Kentucky democrat left his seat in the U.S. Senate for organized baseball's highest post. From that perch he could readily see that the race issue was going to be a major factor in his administration. Indeed, shortly before Chandler took office, a couple of incidents underscored the dangers of continued reluctance to open the doors of Major League Baseball to the black man. Both incidents involved "tryouts" similar to those a few years earlier.

One such incident involved Brooklyn Dodgers president Branch Rickey and took place at the club's upstate New York training camp. Although critical of black sportswriter Joe Bostic's decision to show up, unannounced, with first baseman Dave Thomas and pitcher Terris McDuffie in tow, Rickey allowed the pair to work out for about an hour. Nothing more came of their efforts, but within two years of that gathering Rickey watched Jackie Robinson make his historic first trip to the plate at Ebbets Field.

The other encounter took place in Boston, where the Red Sox warily granted workout privileges to Robinson, already making a name for himself as the Monarchs' second baseman, and two fellow Negro Leaguers: Philadelphia Stars second baseman Marvin Williams and Cleveland Buckeyes center fielder Sam Jethroe. It proved to be a fruitless undertaking. (The Red Sox, in fact, became the last team in the majors to add a black player, Pumpsie Green, in 1959, to its roster.)

Jethroe, a switch-hitting slugger, did eventually make it to "the show" when he signed with Boston's National League franchise, the Braves. In three full seasons with them he hit .261 with 181 runs batted in, 80 doubles, 25 triples, and 49 home runs. Jethroe also led the NL in stolen bases in 1950 and 1951.

It would be Rickey's 1947 Dodgers, however, who took the plunge.

When Rickey left his administrative post with the St. Louis Cardinals in 1942 to take over the Brooklyn ball club, he already was formulating his approach to integrating the game. Knowing that he couldn't rush baseball's power brokers or buck the system, the scholarly Rickey devised a subterfuge that paved the way for black men to enter the majors' ranks.

In 1945 Rickey made an announcement to the press that he was forming a new configuration of black professional baseball teams, the United States League. His scouts, he said, would travel the world, or at least, North America, to sign the best black players they could find to professional contracts. The United States League would be in direct competition with the Negro Leagues.

Of course, Rickey's real motive for creating the new circuit was to throw people off the scent.

Combining scouting reports with his own inquiries, Rickey tentatively decided that Jack Roosevelt Robinson, a twenty-six-year-old former Army lieutenant who earlier had excelled in several sports while attending UCLA, a socially conscious human being who had resisted Jim Crow customs and laws in college and in the Army, and a wise, quick-witted soul betrothed to his college sweetheart, would be the right man to break organized baseball's color barrier.

Outfielder Sam Jethroe as he appeared in a Cleveland Buckeyes uniform. The Boston Braves' first black regular, "Jet" had three good seasons with them in the early 1950s.

**_Two Dodger greats, Jackie Robinson and Branch Rickey,
talk business._**

Japan's agreement to unconditional surrender officially
ended World War II on August 14. Exactly two weeks later a
new battlefront was emerging at Ebbets Field in Brooklyn.
There, inside Rickey's office, the Dodgers' commander in
chief mapped out his strategy for integrating baseball as his
ultimate foot soldier listened intently.

This foot soldier, however, was not to fight. In fact, Rickey
wanted someone who literally as well as figuratively would
turn the other cheek when the enemy taunted him, pushed
him, spiked him, threw at him, ignored him, or talked down
to him.

Rickey assumed a number of universal roles at that August
28 meeting with Robinson: opposing player, teammate, fan,
and other figures who would surely do their damnedest to
make Robinson's life in organized ball a living nightmare.
Showdowns would be never-ending. It was Jackie's difficult
task to make sure he kept his cool and his pride every time he
took the field or stepped up to the plate.

Robinson and Rickey exchanged ideas. They discussed possible scenarios on and off the field. A little personal philosophy was mixed in with the baseball talk. Both men understood what was at stake.

The popular image of the two is that Rickey did all the talking, that Robinson simply sat there and took it all in and then signed a contract to play baseball for the Dodgers' Montreal farm club the next season. But it was a partnership. Rickey and Robinson, Robinson and Rickey—and if Jackie performed well enough in the International League in 1946, he would be brought up to the Dodgers. That was the promise Rickey made to his partner.

Two months later Rickey announced his signing of Robinson to a Triple-A contract. The war to bring racial equality to organized baseball had begun, and people quickly took sides.

Baseball is baseball wherever one goes, but Robinson's season as a Montreal Royal was light-years away from his brief stint as a Kansas City Monarch in the Negro American League. Throughout the International League's host cities, Robinson endured racial epithets yelled at him by fans and bench jockeys, knockdown pitches fired at his head by mean-spirited hurlers, runners who went out of their way to spike his shins or elbow his kidneys, and eateries on the U.S. side that wouldn't serve him. In short, Robinson faced everything Rickey had warned him about, and then some.

Yet despite these mounting external pressures unrelated to the pressures of hitting a curve ball or fielding a hot smash with the game on the line, Jackie Robinson persevered.

Actually, he thrived. He opened the 1946 season by socking a three-run homer, slapping three singles, stealing two bases,

Jackie Robinson sparked the Triple-A Montreal Royals to their Little World Series Championship in 1946. His next stop was superstardom with the Brooklyn Dodgers.

and scoring four runs in a 14–1 "laugher" against Jersey City. He closed the season by getting several clutch hits to help his team win the Little World Series against a tough Louisville Colonels squad. In between these thrilling performances were months of remarkably steady play. When the dust had cleared, Robinson led International League second basemen in fielding percentage, had a league-leading .349 batting average, and had knocked in 113 runs—good enough for a tie at the top in that all-important category.

Still, with all that he accomplished, and despite hitting over .500 against major league pitching in spring training the following year, Robinson was not a shoo-in to make the Dodgers' roster.

First, Rickey had to find a defensive spot for his black pathfinder, so he moved Robinson to first base, not Jackie's normal position but one at which at least four other players saw action in 1946. Rickey did not want to displace any of the Dodger regulars. Had he done so, he would have incurred the wrath of the players and fans alike.

Second, and more importantly, several of Robinson's teammates balked at his presence on the ball club, and drew up a petition stating so. But key players, including Kentuckian Harold "Pee Wee" Reese, the team's acknowledged on-field leader, refused to add their names. Rickey, who understood why some of his protesting players were reacting the way they were, even if he didn't agree with them, promised to trade any player who found it impossible to team with a black man. Although one of the petition instigators, pitcher Kirby Higbe, was traded to Pittsburgh in early May, the others remained with the Dodgers for the 1947 season.

"I first met Jackie and Rachel Robinson in 1947 in Cuba," recalls Buck O'Neil, "right before Jackie made his debut in the Major Leagues. Branch Rickey, I think, wanted the Dodgers to

Swift and evasive Jackie Robinson wasn't always safe at home, but it often seemed that way to the opposition.

hold their spring training in Latin America because racial tolerance was greater down there than it was up here. Maybe he figured it would keep everyone's mind on baseball.

"Anyway, I really liked Jackie. He had all the tools to be a major league baseball player. But he had something else: courage. You could tell he was thinkin' about what would happen if he failed—not so much as an athlete but as a black man in a white man's world—but he somehow managed to behave as just one of the guys tryin' to make the club. He knew, and those of us watchin' him knew, that if his disposition wasn't at just the right pitch, it could've been another twenty, thirty years or more before they would have picked another black man to come up to the big leagues."

As the season progressed, Robinson withstood racial incidents far worse than the one in the Dodgers' clubhouse. Virtually every city the Dodgers visited served up a heaping bowl of abuse. Even during the Dodgers' home stands the visiting players and coaches, feeling smug and secure in the shelter of their dugout, ripped into Robinson with every taunt and insult they could think of. And when word got around that several players on the St. Louis Cardinals might be contemplating a strike to protest Robinson's presence, National League president Ford Frick threatened suspension of any player who pulled such a stunt.

In a repeat of his experiences in the International League the year before, Robinson was kicked, spiked, thrown at, cursed, jeered, defamed, and shunned. He suffered an 0-for-20 slump at the outset of the 1947 season that led some to

Et Tu, Theodore?

Even baseball fans who know little about the game's history can tell you Ted Williams hit .406 in 1941. But did you know he was not the only ballplayer of his generation to accomplish the difficult feat of hitting .400 or better at the professional level? In 1939, twenty-five-year-old "Wild Bill" Wright of the Baltimore Elite Giants led the Negro National League with a .402 batting average. Two years later, Lester Lockett hit .403 for the Birmingham Black Barons of the Negro American League.

question whether Robinson was worth all the turmoil his presence created.

Yet, just as he had for the Royals the year before, Jackie soon responded by getting on base, hitting in the clutch, stealing bases, scoring runs, fielding very well at a new position, and generally galvanizing a Brooklyn club that outplayed both the Cardinals and Braves for the NL pennant. For his first season at organized baseball's highest level, Jackie Robinson hit .297 with 48 RBI, 31 doubles, 5 triples, and 12 home runs. His 29 stolen bases led the National League. He made more than 1,300 putouts and nearly 100 assists at first base while avoiding both the blatant and the subtle attempts to bowl him over or make him bleed.

For his efforts he was voted Major League Baseball's Rookie of the Year by *The Sporting News*. The game's invisible but insidious white wall lay in ruin. Jackie had led the way. Now it was time for others to follow his lead.

But the process was painfully slow that first year.

Bill Veeck, thwarted in his efforts to buy the hapless Phillies, had now assumed ownership of the Cleveland Indians. Veeck brought power-hitting second baseman Larry Doby

Jackie Robinson tries to slide under the tag in an August 1953 game at the Polo Grounds against the Giants.

from the Newark Eagles directly to the Indians—no minor league stops along the way. (Doby hit just .156 in about 30 games, but was converted to a center fielder for the Indians' 1948 campaign and hit .301 with 14 homers and 66 RBI in only 121 games as he played an integral part in the team's successful pennant drive.)

The Dodgers, meanwhile, signed another former Negro Leaguer, pitcher Dan Bankhead, at the tail end of August. He pitched sparingly, and had no decisions that year, but he did earn the distinction of being the first black pitcher to appear in the majors. Bankhead's best season was 1950, when he divided his time between starting and relieving, going 9–4 for a Dodger team that also featured Jackie Robinson, Roy Campanella, and Don Newcombe—four black players who at various times in their professional careers had honed their talents in the Negro Leagues.

Although more and more Negro Leaguers entered the minors with their sights set on the majors, few big-league organizations were actively pursuing black talent. Still, that gritty coterie of Robinson and the others set high standards for those who followed.

In addition to the Dodgers' foursome, other onetime Negro Leaguers who enjoyed varying degrees of success at the big-league level include Larry Doby and Satchel Paige with the Indians; Monte Irvin, Willie Mays, and Hank Thompson with the New York Giants; Sam Jethroe with the Boston Braves; Minnie Minoso with the White Sox; Ernie Banks and Gene Baker with the Cubs; Hank Aaron with the Milwaukee Braves; Bob Thurman with the Cincinnati Reds; and Joe Black, also

Former Newark Eagle Larry Doby, the American League's first black player, helped the Cleveland Indians win pennants in 1948 and 1954 with his power and defensive skills.

Baseball instantly became a better game when blacks were given an opportunity to show their hustle, determination, and smarts to their white peers. This foursome of Roy Campanella, Larry Doby, Joe Black, and Jackie Robinson was part of the first wave of talented players to make the transition from the Negro Leagues to the major leagues.

with the Dodgers. This is by no means a complete list of former Negro Leaguers who earned their shot at the majors; it should indicate, however, the caliber of player that black professional baseball produced.

As Ted Radcliffe, whose nickname, "Double Duty," was coined decades ago by journalist Damon Runyon after the scribe saw Radcliffe catch for Paige in the first game of a Negro League doubleheader and then take the mound to pitch the nightcap, says of the Negro Leagues:

"We played an exciting brand of baseball, and we entertained the people who came to see us play. But we weren't entertaining 'cause we were clownin' around out there. No sir. We were entertaining 'cause we took the game seriously and played good, solid, *professional* baseball.

Monte Irvin was thirty-three when he socked this triple against the Pittsburgh Pirates. Elected to the Hall of Fame on the basis of his career in the Negro Leagues, Irvin is now a spokesman for the Negro League Baseball Players Association.

"Those big-league teams knew that. If we hadn't put out our best effort on the field, they never would have looked at us."

Sadly, many of the Negro Leagues' greatest players were past their prime when Robinson broke the color line. Once denied entry because of their skin color, they were now disregarded because of their age. And some legends, including Rube Foster and Josh Gibson, died before they could witness Robinson's historic debut with the Dodgers on April 15, 1947.

Gibson's untimely death in January of that year is remembered by a teammate, Bob Thurman, who played with Josh on the Homestead Grays:

Roy Campanella (left) was a three-time National League MVP. Willard Brown (above, left) and Hank Thompson (above, right) also reached the majors, though only Thompson—with the N.Y. Giants—made a name for himself.

"Just in the short time I knew him, we became buddies. Real good buddies. I think it was in my first game with the Grays, in front of about 4,000 people at Griffith Stadium in Washington, D.C., and I hit a ball *downtown*. I mean, I creamed it, and that ballpark was not an easy one to hit home runs in, either. Josh was the first man to greet me at the plate.

"He said, 'Bob! Bob! You can hit a ball as far as I can!' And he and I laughed and laughed. After the game he took me to one of his favorite joints for a few drinks. He introduced me to everybody there, tellin' 'em how I could hit a ball as far as he could. He was a tough ballplayer…strong…but good-natured, you know? A real nice guy. Always makin' his teammates feel important.

"During the winter of '46–'47, Josh asked me if I wanted to go to L.A. with him on some business. He told me he was goin' in about ten days or so, and I said, 'Just let me know what day you're comin' and I'll be ready.' I had heard that he'd been sick in the past, but I still couldn't believe it when I read the paper a week or two later that said Josh had died. Oh, brother, I thought, how can that be? He was still a young man. But I'll never forget him. None of us who knew him or saw him play will ever forget Josh Gibson."

The debuts of Robinson, Doby, Bankhead, and Thompson in 1947 and the debuts of Paige and Campanella in 1948 were more an anomaly than the start of a widespread rush of black players to hit the majors. Even though big-league clubs were tapping the Negro Leagues, they failed to open the sluice valve and let the talent really flow.

Every year, a few more clubs would sign one or two black players. Whether these men eventually made a club's big-league roster or were sent to the minor leagues, where the level of competition was less formidable than what they'd experienced in the Negro Leagues, these moves were often

Above: Josh Gibson eyes the plate after creaming a pitch in cavernous Griffith Stadium in 1942. Opposite page: Twenty-five years later, Chicago Cubs slugger Ernie Banks creams his second homer of the game against the Houston Astros in "the Friendly Confines."

nothing more than an attempt to placate the critics who accused major league teams of Jim Crowism. It wasn't uncommon for black players to be signed to a contract and then forced to "ride the pines" in the dugout. They suffered in silence while seeing little playing time.

There were exceptions to this, of course. Former Homestead Gray and Kansas City Monarch Bob Thurman says he saw quite a lot of action when he played in the minors. In fact, Thurman says an incident in the Reds' minor league system was instrumental in the parent club's decision to bring him up in 1955. Thurman, the Reds' brass reasoned, had what it took to make it in the majors.

"A big ol' white boy was on the mound for the other team," Thurman begins, "and me bein' the only black ballplayer out there for either team, he decided he would test me. He knocked me down on the first pitch. Threw a fastball straight at my head. The pitch separated me from my cap, and I hit the dirt so fast I was a blur.

"Didn't matter what color the pitcher was—white or black—I never got mad when stuff like that happened. I just got up, dusted myself off, and told the catcher and the umpire that before this game was over I was gonna hit a pitch right back at that clown. I was primed, boy, let me tell you. Well, during this very same at bat, as it turned out, I got just the right pitch, and I hit a line drive so hard that the ball went between the pitcher's legs, hit the pitching rubber and went *boing!* and bounced out to center field on one bounce, where the center fielder grabbed it and tossed it in to the shortstop.

"The fans started laughin', and when I stood on the bag at first base, I just looked over at the pitcher and gave him that 'neck thing'—you know, where I moved my finger across my throat to let him know if he threw at me again I was gonna hit the next pitch so hard that it'd cut his head off. Well, he was red as a beet, either from him bein' angry or embarrassed or both, I'm not sure which. And he glared at me, but he never did throw at me again."

Sadly, even with the initial successes of Robinson and other former Negro Leaguers, and the soon-to-follow achievements of Ernie Banks, Hank Aaron, and Minnie Minoso, it wasn't until 1959 that the last of the period's sixteen major league teams had integrated its roster, and not until two years later that every team had at least one black among its regulars.

Yet the influx of blacks to the professional ranks of the big leagues, slow as it was, sapped the Negro Leagues of many of their star athletes. Without people like Robinson, Campanella, and the others, interest in Negro League baseball saw a marked decline at the turnstiles. Notably in cities that sported both a major league team and a Negro League team, attendance dropped at Negro League contests. Fans of black baseball were now more inclined to catch a big-league game than they were a Negro League game.

"Bill Veeck and Branch Rickey may have been Good Samaritans; they may have had the right intentions, the best intentions, to bring about integration of the then all-white major leagues," says Negro Leagues researcher Larry Lester, "but they also were smart businessmen who knew that black ballplayers—and the quality of baseball being played at that time in the Negro Leagues—would put fans in the seats of the big-league ballparks.

"So their push for integrating the big leagues may have been a financial consideration as much as a testimony for civil rights. But whatever their intentions were, it was important that integration of the majors came about."

Indeed, integration of the majors was important even to the owners of Negro League teams, who stood to lose the most from it. Although these owners wanted to continue their operations, they, like the players under contract with them, desired integration of the majors. To help bolster their clubs' faltering financial situations, Negro League team owners were forced to sell some of their better players to the big-league franchises for what little money the white owners offered, which was usually no more than several thousand dollars. (Branch Rickey didn't pay the Monarchs a cent for Jackie Robinson.)

"When I returned to the U.S. after serving with the Navy in the Philippines from '43 through '45," recalls Buck O'Neil, "I was still a full-time player for the Monarchs. I started cutting down on my playing time in 1948 and began managing the ball club. By that time, we were concentrating more on developing our younger players for the major leagues than we were on winning Negro League pennants. It was the only way we could stay in business."

One truly magical moment came on the night of April 8, 1974, when Atlanta Brave Hank Aaron socked his 715th career home run—a new major league record.

Bobby Robinson

The second best-known export from Whistler, Alabama, was Bobby Robinson, a talented third baseman for several Negro League teams in the 1920s, 30s, and 40s. Robinson's glovework earned him the respect of his fellow professionals, both black and white. In a playoff game against the St. Louis Stars in 1930, Robinson (then with the Detroit Stars) backhanded a hot liner off his shoe tops, tagged "Cool Papa" Bell while lunging back to third base for a second out, and fired the ball to Grady Orange, who was covering second base, to complete a triple play. Several members of the New York Giants—enjoying an off-day before their series with the hometown St. Louis Cardinals —witnessed the thrilling sequence. They invited Bobby over to their box seats along the third base line before Detroit came to bat. Bobby was greeted by handshakes, backslapping, and spirited congratulations by the white ballplayers, including Giants' first baseman Bill Terry, who told Robinson it was the first time in his fifteen-year professional career he'd seen a team turn a triple play. (And who was the best-known export from Whistler, Alabama? Hall of Famer and former Cubs great Billy Williams, whose father, Frank, played ball in his younger days with none other than fishing and hunting pal, Bobby Robinson.)

In 1981 Rube Foster, the "Father of Black Baseball," was finally inducted into the National Baseball Hall of Fame. Known as a fair arbiter, an outstanding athlete, and someone who demanded excellence from every player (whether or not from his team, the Chicago American Giants), Foster presided over the first Negro National League. He is indisputably one of the most significant figures in the history of baseball.

The double whammy of declining attendance and losing their star players to the major and minor leagues was too much for the Negro Leagues. A few teams ceased operations entirely. Others opted for a return to their barnstorming days. There was even an attempt by some proponents of Negro League baseball to have black clubs serve as minor league outposts for white big-league teams, but that idea quickly fizzled.

Hundreds of black ballplayers found themselves in a no-win situation. Making a decent living playing ball in the Negro Leagues had always been a fragile proposition, but now many players were jobless because the owners couldn't keep their clubs afloat.

By the early 1950s the Negro National League was finished and the Negro American League was a weak configuration of fewer than eight teams. Negro League baseball lasted into the early 1960s, but by then few people really cared. The top black stars of the day were making noise in the big leagues.

The final East-West All-Star Game was held in 1963 in Kansas City—fitting, perhaps, since that was where Rube Foster and his fellow pioneers organized the first black professional baseball league almost forty-five years before.

Interestingly, the man whose courage, skill, and intellect knocked a gaping hole in the game's racial barrier did not recall his days in the Negro Leagues kindly. Jackie Robinson gave little credit to the leagues and his stint with the Kansas City Monarchs for his success in the big leagues, and generally dwelled on the negative aspects of life in black professional baseball. But Robinson and other former Negro Leaguers who ascended to the majors owed a great deal to black baseball.

It was there that they honed their skills while awaiting the day for big-league baseball to beckon to them.

Jackie Robinson (kneeling, second from left) played briefly with the Kansas City Monarchs before making history in the major leagues.

Chapter 7:

Hanging Up The Spikes

ven when the men of the Negro Leagues retired from the playing ranks, they didn't really divorce themselves from the game they loved. Some stayed on in a coaching or managing capacity in the Negro Leagues. Others tried to coax their bodies into playing one or two more seasons in semi-pro ball. Some played or coached baseball in Latin America, often making their permanent homes there. A handful switched uniforms and became umpires at the professional or amateur level.

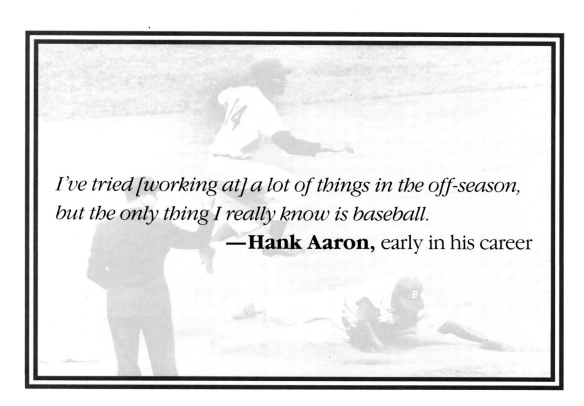

I've tried [working at] a lot of things in the off-season, but the only thing I really know is baseball.
—**Hank Aaron,** early in his career

There were even a select few, such as Buck O'Neil, who were hired as big-league scouts. O'Neil, in fact, was the man who signed former Monarchs player Ernie Banks to a contract with the Chicago Cubs. O'Neil later became the big leagues' first black coach when he donned a Cub uniform in 1962.

A former Negro Leaguer who made it to "the show" as a player and later scouted future major league talent was Bob Thurman. Thurman served as a special assignment scout for a dozen big-league clubs for many years. He was instrumental in signing future Hall of Fame catcher Johnny Bench to a contract with the Cincinnati Reds.

Regardless of who they were or where they wound up, Negro Leaguers had a tradition of passing their knowledge on to those who would take the time to watch and listen. Even when they were still active, veteran players in the Negro Leagues took it upon themselves to teach the up-and-comers. The instruction they offered and the baseball smarts they pos-

sessed were invaluable. It was the kind of personal attention one can't derive from studying a how-to manual, reading a book, or watching others take batting practice.

O'Neil was there for the kids. So was Thurman. Satchel Paige, Connie Johnson, and Woody Smallwood were, too. Chet Brewer was an outstanding instructor once his glory days came to a close. Over the years dozens upon dozens of Negro Leaguers have shared their knowledge with young players eager to learn baseball from the men who excelled at it when the game was segregated into all-black and all-white professional leagues.

There is a telling story of a game years ago involving a team of Negro Leaguers competing against a team of talented young amateurs. It happened in front of a large crowd of fans:

Opposite page: DeWitt "Woody" Smallwood was one of many superb Negro Leaguers; in 1992 he was president of the Negro Leagues Baseball Museum in Kansas City.

Negro-Leaguers-turned-major-leaguers Monte Irvin (left) and Larry Doby (right) played integral parts in their teams'
successes in the 1950s—Irvin with the N.Y. Giants and Doby with the Cleveland Indians.

One of the Negro Leaguers was rounding third and barreling toward home plate as the teenage catcher braced himself for a collision while awaiting his outfielder's throw. A few feet from the plate the runner stopped dead in his tracks and yelled at the dumbfounded catcher holding the ball.

"Wait a minute, son. Don't tag me out like you were gonna do just now, 'cause I'll hurt you."

As the fans watched in amazement, the runner allowed himself to be tagged "out" and then took the catcher by the arm and positioned him properly for nailing any future runners charging toward home.

"You do it this way, and you'll be doing it the right way," the Negro Leaguer said. Then, without missing a beat, he laughed and said, "'Course, I won't be slowin' down next time. I plan to try and knock you on your butt."

On another occasion, a young Chuck Dobson, who would go on to enjoy a successful big-league career with the Athletics and the Angels from 1966 through 1975, learned firsthand that a blazing, "unhittable" fastball isn't always the right choice against a wily veteran.

Dobson, a white man, was pitching for an integrated squad of young all-stars when they faced a team of former Negro Leaguers who supposedly were well past their prime. Alfred "Slick" Surratt and Hank Bayless were members of this "Over the Hill Gang."

Dobson fired a fastball that caught the inside corner of the plate for a called strike. Bayless jumped back as if he were afraid of the ball that had just whistled past him. Dobson smiled.

A Rookie at Age Thirty

Year after year, Monte Irvin was a "do-it-all" player for the Newark Eagles of the Negro National League. He could hit, hit with power, run, throw, and field. But year after year he was passed over for other black ballplayers as the majors' color barrier crumbled. When Irvin did get the call in 1949 he was thirty years old, hardly the time in one's life to break into the big leagues. But by the following year Irvin had established himself as a hitter to be reckoned with. And in the New York Giants' memorable pennant drive of 1951, Irvin was a key man at the plate, knocking in a league-leading 121 runs while batting .312 with 24 home runs, 11 triples, and 19 doubles. Monte's lifetime stats for an eight-year big-league career include a .293 batting average, 443 RBI, and 99 home runs. What might he have accomplished had he been given the chance to play in the majors when he was in his twenties?

Satchel Paige was one of many Negro Leaguers who over the years offered free advice to youngsters who dreamed of a career in professional baseball. When "ol' Satch" spoke, the kids listened.

He could hear his coaches yelling, "Don't throw him that again!" But before their words could sink in, Dobson was already bringing another blazing fastball homeward toward the "timid" Bayless.

Bayless hit the ball so hard, says one observer, that "it damn near landed on the interstate some four hundred feet away." Bayless chuckled to himself as he circled the bases for a home run.

Dobson, shocked that his second serving traveled so far, bore down, determined to show everyone Bayless' home run was a fluke. But Dobson was clobbered pretty hard by the former Negro Leaguers. A few walks, several hits, and a couple of runs later, Dobson put his hands on his hips, looked toward his dugout, and shouted in frustration, "Coach! Coach! How do I get these old men out?"

Bayless talked to Dobson later in the game and said, "You never try to run just fastballs by a good hitter. What you try to do is outthink him."

Dobson's coach in the Ban Johnson League, Don Motley, says of that incident, "Chuck Dobson will tell you today that that's how he learned to pitch in order to make the big leagues."

Satchel Paige often combined his instruction with a bit of showmanship. Paige would take a slip of paper and place it lengthwise across home plate, anchoring the paper with a few pebbles. Taking his position on the mound, he proceeded to fire pitch after pitch directly over that slip of paper. Anyone who can do that, a longtime Paige observer says, "commands your immediate attention."

Motley says Paige would often call and ask if there were any of his young charges who might want to learn a few things about good pitching and, by association, good hitting. Other Negro Leaguers offered their services as well. These mini-camps, Motley says, were of great benefit to his players.

The Negro Leaguers cherished the game to which they had given so much for so long. Even after they had physically hung up their spikes for good, mentally and emotionally they were still suiting up for the next game. Like many other former athletes—whatever their color or background or social standing—Negro Leaguers always get that special look on their faces when they recount their playing days.

But there was life after black baseball. There had to be. These men and their families had to eat. The former Negro Leaguers had to move on, and the jobs they took were as varied as one might imagine.

Some, like George Giles, who owned and operated a bar and restaurant, entered the business world. Others, like pitcher Connie Johnson and umpire Bob Motley, were gainfully employed at various automotive plants in the Midwest.

Outfielder–first baseman Armando Vazquez has been a custodian in the New York school system for many years; at one time, Vazquez was volunteering his time to work with handicapped children.

In the late 1960s, Monte Irvin joined the advisory staff of Baseball Commissioner Bowie Kuhn. Willie Mays served as a big-league batting instructor. Hank Aaron is senior vice president of the Atlanta Braves and an assistant to club president Stan Kasten.

Postal workers. Security guards. Teachers. Pages. Cabbies. Public relations advisors. Bus drivers. You name the job or career, and at least one former Negro Leaguer probably held it.

"It wasn't always easy for us to make the transition once we got out of the game," one former Negro Leaguer says. "But somehow we managed. We faced prejudice and hardships in white society.

"Some of us fared better than others. Some of us died young, died before our time, really. But we always had that one thing we shared in common: we were professional ballplayers, and Lord, how we loved the game."

Former N.Y. Giants manager Leo Durocher always wore his 1954 World Series ring. A few years before his death, Leo said of Willie Mays, "And he helped me get it."

Appendix:
Respect, Redemption, Recognition

The young black man stood and gazed at the street sign. It read: J "Cool-Papa" Bell Ave.

A bright young man who also excelled at baseball was in search of James "Cool Papa" Bell, a legendary ballplayer from the Negro Leagues. The young man modeled his game after Bell's: use one's speed to take advantage of the other team's weaknesses; steal a base; bunt for a hit; stretch a single into a double; make things happen.

The eighty-year-old Bell was living in poverty in a St. Louis ghetto on a short, one-way street named for him. The newcomer spotted an energetic black child playing on the nearly deserted pavement and asked the child about the sign.

"Do you know who that is, the man whose name is on that street sign?"

"No, I don't know who he is," came the soft reply.

"Don't you live around here?"

"Yeah, I live right over here on this street, but I don't know who that is."

"He lives in that house right over there," the young man said, pointing in the direction of a small home several feet away.

"No kidding?" was the child's only response, as he resumed his outdoor play, uninterested in pursuing the conversation.

Undaunted, the visiting hero-worshiper stepped up to the old gentleman's front door and knocked. Taking off several locks and dead bolts, Bell opened the door and greeted his visitor with a warm smile as he led him into the living room.

I remember my first baseball uniform many years ago when I was a kid. I was so happy, I slept in it the night before we played a Sunday game.
—Armando Vazquez, a teammate of Hank Aaron at Indianapolis of the Negro American League

Once inside, the young man saw more trophies, plaques, pictures, and other baseball memorabilia than there were pieces of furniture.

Had Mr. Bell been white, the visitor thought to himself, he would not be living in poverty like this. The autographs on the baseballs alone would bring "Cool Papa" a cool sum that could pay for his rent, yet here was this baseball legend—a man enshrined in the National Baseball Hall of Fame even though he played his entire career in the Negro Leagues when organized baseball quietly but effectively kept blacks out of its ranks—struggling to make ends meet.

Even in his own neighborhood, on a street named in his honor, people didn't know much about James "Cool Papa" Bell. But the visitor did, and that day he spent one of the more

Opposite page: In his later years, "Cool Papa" Bell lived on a relatively little-known street named in his honor. Bell epitomized the daring but smart style of play that characterized the Negro Leagues.

Southpaw Dave Brown keyed the Chicago American Giants' successes in the early 1920s. He got into trouble with the law and by late 1924 had disappeared from sight.

Another Negro Leaguer was usually compared to baseball immortal Lou Gehrig, but Jud Nelson's screaming low liners to the gap certainly reminded people of Gehrig's cannon shots.

One wouldn't think so from looking at pictures of him, but slugger Oscar Charleston was surprisingly fast. Many of his contemporaries said he was the best ballplayer they ever saw.

Illustrations © Mark Chiarello

memorable afternoons of his young life talking baseball with his hero and wondering why a man of Bell's stature had been virtually forgotten in his waning years.

A decade later, at a well-attended baseball card and memorabilia show in suburban Chicago, about fifteen former Negro Leaguers gathered to sign autographs for collectors and fans alike. Three of the men, Monte Irvin, Ernie Banks, and Willie Mays, went on to greatness in the major leagues. Otherwise, the handwritten name cards on the thirty-foot table meant little to the autograph hunters.

Who are these guys? What teams did they play for? Where did they play? When did they play? Did they do anything

great? The soft-spoken comments among those in attendance clearly indicated the identity crisis still facing the men of the Negro Leagues.

Episodes like those in St. Louis and Chicago are not isolated ones. Negro League baseball is a subject that people probably misunderstand or ignore, or both, more than any other aspect of the game's history. If it didn't happen in the majors, it must not have been very good, the faulty reasoning goes.

But the caliber of play in the Negro Leagues was never in question during their heyday. Just as important is the idea that black professional baseball not only served as the breeding ground for such future big-league stars and superstars as Hank

Aaron, Roy Campanella, Satchel Paige, and the aforementioned trio of Irvin, Banks, and Mays, but introduced creative, run-producing plays and contributed several important inventions—shin guards for catchers, batting helmets for hitters, night baseball for fans, to name just three—to the national pastime.

"That's why it's so important to have a museum where these men can be honored," explains Negro Leagues researcher Larry Lester, who ten years ago visited his hero, "Cool Papa" Bell, at his St. Louis home.

"We want to educate people, particularly the kids—black *and* white—that there are other great heroes of baseball besides the major league ballplayers who are always getting promoted in one way or another. The Negro Leaguers, despite a few being in the Hall of Fame at Cooperstown, have been swept under the rug and forgotten."

The idea behind the Negro Leagues Baseball Museum, which at this point is a second-floor office in a beautifully refurbished building in Kansas City's historic 18th and Vine District, is to promote a better understanding of the leagues and emphasize their history and their value to baseball.

The Negro Leagues offer a wealth of new stories, new memories, and new excitement just waiting to be discovered and shared by people of all races and ages. Along with this exciting discovery comes the realization that America is only about one hundred and fifty obituaries away from losing this part of its history forever. Now is the time, stress proponents of the museum, for recognizing the living members of the Negro Leagues while honoring those who have passed away in relative obscurity.

"Tomorrow is not promised to anyone," Lester says. "Every day that one of these former Negro Leaguers lives beyond the age of sixty-five, which is a long time for a black man to live if

Many players in the Negro Leagues could handle several positions, and handle them well. Josh Johnson was such a player. Doubling as a catcher and pitcher for the Cincinnati Tigers, Homestead Grays, and New York Black Yankees, Johnson was a fixture of the Negro Leagues in the late 1930s.

Is This All There Is?

Only eleven men enshrined in the National Baseball Hall of Fame and Museum are so honored based on their accomplishments in the Negro Leagues. The first to be elected was Satchel Paige, in 1971; Ray Dandridge was the last, in 1987. Despite efforts by a variety of groups and individual supporters to get other worthy Negro Leaguers immortalized at Cooperstown, it may take a concerted push by the media, the nation's fans, and savvy baseball researchers to force the Hall of Fame's Veterans Committee, which considers former players, coaches, managers, umpires, and executives not voted in by the Baseball Writers Association of America, to answer the question "Out of the many hundreds of smart, talented Negro Leaguers who played in the 1920s, 30s, 40s, or 50s, is this group of eleven all there is to be inducted?"

Ray Dandridge, the last Negro Leaguer to be elected to the Hall of Fame, lunges for a ball.

you go by today's actuarial tables, we are blessed by his presence. It's important to build a real museum now, while these men are alive."

Plans call for interpretive exhibits, where visitors can push a button and see and hear audiovisual presentations of the greats and near-greats, living and dead, talking about their careers or serving up a few choice anecdotes about life in the Negro Leagues.

There is to be a special room honoring Jackie Robinson, the man who made a difference in 1947, when big-league baseball still wasn't sure it wanted integration, and similar rooms devoted to the lives and times of Josh Gibson, "Cool Papa" Bell, Satchel Paige, and Rube Foster.

Still other areas of the museum will spotlight the history and importance of the annual East-West All-Star Game, the Negro League World Series, and the uniforms and equipment of the Negro Leaguers.

There has even been talk of constructing a batting cage and a bullpen, where high school and college coaches can bring their players to receive instruction from former Negro Leaguers and major leaguers alike who still live in the Kansas City area.

In addition, museum organizers are mulling over the idea of presenting annual awards to spotlight specific accomplishments. The award for community achievement, for example, would be named in honor of former Negro League pitching great and minor league coach Chet Brewer. An award named in honor of Rube Foster would go to the top baseball executive in the country. A separate award would go to the top researcher of the Negro Leagues, and be named the Sol White Award in honor of the former player and social commentator who wrote the first history of the Negro Leagues back around the turn of the century.

Negro Leaguers such as Satchel Paige (right) subsidized their earnings both with exhibition games and with barnstorming tours against the likes of Dizzy Dean (center) and Cecil Travis (left).

I Gotta Hit It *How* Far?

Among the common misconceptions some people have of the Negro Leagues is that the ballparks were nothing more than bandboxes and that any claim of a "prodigious home run blast" should be taken with a grain of salt. This is not so. Over the years, several teams in the Negro Leagues played their home games in major league ballparks such as Yankee Stadium. And of course, the East-West All-Star Game was held in Comiskey Park in Chicago every year. Ballparks built specifically for black professional baseball clubs were anything but a cinch for the batters. In Philip J. Lowry's wonderfully detailed book *Green Cathedrals*, the author notes that at one Negro League ballpark the distance from home plate to centerfield was 470 feet (143m); at another, 512 feet (156m); and at a third, a whopping 600 feet (182m). At that last one, even "pull" hitters had to hope for a swift air current—it was 420 feet (128m) down the left field line and 600 feet (182m) down the right field line.

Above and opposite page: Comiskey Park in Chicago was home to the East-West All-Star game, the crown jewel of black professional baseball. Below: The 1948 East squad included Minnie Minoso (kneeling, sixth from left), who would later play in Comiskey Park as a star member of the "Go-Go" White Sox of the 1950s.

East West Game
Comiskey Park
Chicago Ill
Aug 6-193?

"We want to promote the wearing of Negro League apparel," Lester adds, "so that all Americans can feel a sense of pride when they don a cap or jersey of the Birmingham Black Barons, the Memphis Red Sox, or the Pittsburgh Crawfords. It'll be something different from the usual spate of Chicago Bulls, Dallas Cowboys, or New York Mets items that you see practically wherever you go."

Obtaining a licensing agreement with certain manufacturers will provide the museum with much-needed revenue to help maintain a quality museum and channel some of the money to those players still living.

"Here you have these former players, managers, coaches, and umpires who labored in obscurity during their careers, and who are still relatively unknown," Lester says.

"They draw no pension, have no plaques of their own hanging in Cooperstown, don't get invited to many card shows or other public functions where baseball honors its past, and they are often struggling financially. Our goal is to honor them with what I call baseball's *real* Triple Crown: respect, redemption, and recognition."

Plans call for the Negro Leagues Baseball Museum to be part of a complex that also will house the International Jazz Hall of Fame and the Black Archives of Mid-America. The complex is to be built at the southern tip of Kansas City's Parade Park, literally a stone's throw away from I–70.

The Kansas City Office of Housing and Community Development points out that dozens of other landmarks are situated in the historic 18th and Vine District, including the Monarchs' Baseball Club office, the Eblon Theater, William "Count" Basie's residence, the Centennial United Methodist Church, and Lucille's Paradise Band Box, where the legendary Charlie "Bird" Parker briefly played before making his mark in Chicago and elsewhere.

City officials have allocated $20 million for the project, but outside funding is crucial to the success of such an ambitious not-for-profit organization.

"I envision this museum as being more than a place where people come in and stare at pictures on a wall or bats behind a Plexiglas display," says executive director Don Motley. "I see this as a living history museum, where the people interact with their surroundings. I want visitors to be able to *do* things once they come inside.

"What I *don't* want is for this museum, or any part of the proposed complex, to turn into a twenty-eight-day exhibit in February when people feel obligated to celebrate Black History Month. And working, as I have, with young people for over forty years in Ban Johnson and American Legion baseball, I can tell you that this will be the ideal place for youngsters of all races to come and learn something about a little-known and underappreciated aspect of American history. Baseball is the American game."

Above: The mighty Pittsburgh Crawfords of 1935 included such greats as Judy Johnson (top row, second from left), Josh Gibson (top row, second from right), and "Cool Papa" Bell (middle row, far left). Opposite page: Buck O'Neil spends a quiet moment in the pen.

Negro Leagues Timeline

1867: Three years into the country's Reconstruction period—a time when the United States attempted to heal the self-inflicted social, political, and economic wounds from the Civil War—the National Association of Base Ball Players votes to disbar all blacks from participating in its newly formed professional league.

1872: With his debut on an all-white team in western Pennsylvania, John "Bud" Fowler—a native of Cooperstown, NY—becomes the man now considered the first black professional baseball player. His career included stints in the Western League and the International League, as well as years of barnstorming.

1879: Andrew "Rube" Foster is born on September 17 in Calvert, Texas. Foster, a superb pitcher in his younger days, goes on to organize the Negro National League (NNL) and establish a positive environment for black athletes to learn their craft.

1884: Moses Fleetwood "Fleet" Walker becomes the first black major leaguer when he signs on as a catcher with Toledo of the American Association. His younger brother, Weldy, an outfielder, plays occasionally for the team.

1887: The International League decides it no longer wants to be interracial, and officials establish a ban on all future contracts with blacks. The so-called "color line" is drawn. Many all-black professional teams continue to participate in the national pastime, however, and compete against white teams.

1898: The last traces of black players in organized baseball die out when the Acme Colored Giants shuts down operations in mid-season.

1907: Sol White, a black professional ballplayer turned journalist, publishes *The History of Colored Base Ball*, the first account of early black players' experiences in and contributions to the game of baseball.

1919: Jack Roosevelt Robinson is born on January 31 in Cairo, Georgia. "Jackie" makes American history when he debuts in a Brooklyn Dodgers uniform twenty-eight years later.

1920: The Negro National League, a group of eight ballclubs based in the Midwest and the game's first truly successful black professional league, opens its turnstiles. The league flourishes for about a dozen years before it folds.

1923: A second assembly of black professional ballclubs, the Eastern Colored League (ECL), begins operations. By the early 1930s, it, too, is gone.

1924: The first all-black World Series takes place between the Kansas City Monarchs of the NNL and the Hilldale club of the ECL. The Monarchs, keyed by the pitching performances of Wilbur "Bullet" Rogan and Jose Mendez, defeat Hilldale, 5 games to 4, in a series that features games played not only in the home cities of the two rival clubs, but in Baltimore and Chicago, too.

1930: Baseball under the lights hits the big time when the Phillips University baseball squad and the J.L. Wilkinson–owned Kansas City Monarchs of the NNL face each other in an exhibition game featuring portable artificial lighting developed by Wilkinson and business partner Tom Baird. This innovation helps the Negro Leagues to endure tough economic times, and permanent artificial lighting is adopted by Major League Baseball several years later.

1933: Gus Greenlee establishes a new version of the Negro National League. Like its predecessor, it flourishes for more than a dozen years.

1933: The first East-West All-Star Game pitting two teams of the nation's top Negro Leaguers against each other is played in Comiskey Park, the home of the Chicago White Sox and the site of the first Major League All-Star Game earlier that summer. The West squad beats the East squad 11–7. Year after year, the East-West contest proves to be bigger than the Colored World Series. By the 1940s the annual event is drawing more than its white counterpart.

1944: Albert B. "Happy" Chandler succeeds Kenesaw Mountain Landis as Commissioner of Baseball. Chandler is open to the idea of permitting blacks to play in the majors, a key difference between the two men.

1947: On the afternoon of April 15, Jackie Robinson, twenty-eight, assumes his batting stance at home plate in Ebbets Field. Baseball's color line is finally broken as the game—and perhaps much of America itself—slowly but promisingly enters a new era. Though hitless in three at bats, the speedy Robinson sparks the Dodgers' come-from-behind victory when his sacrifice bunt attempt in the bottom of the seventh is mishandled by Braves pitcher Earl Torgeson. Three Brooklyn runners, including Robinson, eventually cross the plate that inning as the Dodgers win 5–3 on Opening Day. He is named 1947's "Rookie of the Year" by *The Sporting News*.

1948: Larry Doby, who made his big-league debut with the Cleveland Indians in 1947 about three months after Robinson made his debut with Brooklyn, helps lead his team to its first American League pennant and World Championship in nearly thirty years.

1951: As the decade of the 50s moves ahead, more and more black players begin to grace big-league baseball. Many of the better players coming into their own at this time, including Willie Mays, Hank Aaron, Ernie Banks, Monte Irvin, and Minnie Minoso, had their starts in the Negro Leagues. (And of course, the venerable Satchel Paige, who managed to go 12–10 for the lowly St. Louis Browns in 1952, was a mainstay of black professional baseball for decades before signing with Cleveland for the 1948 season.)

1962: Jackie Robinson, who socked the cover off the ball for the Kansas City Monarchs one season in the 1940s before advancing to the Triple-A and major-league levels of professional baseball, is inducted into the National Baseball Hall of Fame and Museum at Cooperstown, N.Y., the hometown of Bud Fowler, the man generally regarded as the first black pro baseball player.

Bibliography

The following books and publications were used as background sources for this pictorial history:

Carter, Craig, ed. *Daguerreotypes* 8th ed. St. Louis: The Sporting News
    Publishing Co., 1990.

Conrads, David. "A Natural." *Kansas City Live!* February 1992.

Craft, David, and Tom Owens. *Redbirds Revisited: Great Memories and Stories from
    St. Louis Cardinals.* Chicago: Bonus Books, 1990.

Dickson, Paul. *Baseball's Greatest Quotations.* New York: HarperPerennial Edition, 1992.

Holway, John B. *Blackball Stars: Negro League Pioneers.* New York: Carroll & Graf, 1992.

Negro Leagues Baseball Museum. "John 'Buck' O'Neil: 80th Birthday" program.
    Kansas City, Mo. Negro Leagues Baseball Museum, Nov. 16, 1991.

Peterson, Robert. *Only The Ball Was White.* New York: McGraw-Hill, 1984.

Rogosin, Donn. *Invisible Men: Life In Baseball's Negro Leagues.* New York:
    Atheneum, 1983.

Tygiel, Jules. *Baseball's Great Experiment: Jackie Robinson And His Legacy.* New York:
    Vintage Books, 1984.

Veeck, Bill, and Ed Linn. *Veeck—As In Wreck.* New York: Holtzman Press Inc., 1962.

Photo Credits

**National Baseball Library/Cooperstown,
NY:** 2, 10–11, 13, 15, 20, 22, 23, 25, 26 (all), 32,
35, 36, 37, 38, 40, 41, 41 (middle), 42, 43, 45,
46 (top), 47, 49, 51, 52, 53, 57, 60, 61, 62, 63,
64, 65 (both), 66 (both), 68, 69, 70, 71, 72, 73,
74, 75, 76, 77, 78, 78–79, 80, 81, 82, 83, 84,
85 (both), 86, 87, 89, 90 (both), 91, 93, 94, 95,
96, 97 (bottom), 98, 101, 102, 103, 104 (top),
105, 107, 108–109

**Negro Leagues Baseball Museum/Kansas
City, MO:** 4, 12, 14, 17, 18, 21, 24, 28 (center),
30, 31, 34, 39, 48, 54–55, 56, 58, 59, 67, 86,
92, 106

FPG International/New York, NY: 26,
28–29, 46, 85 (left)

Rod Shelley: 2, 28 (mitts), 50 (pennants),
51 (pennants), 97 (pennant), 103

© **Mark Chiarello:** 6 (all), 16 (pennants),
19, 100 (all)

Associated Organizations

Negro Leagues Baseball Museum
1601 East 18th Street, Suite 260
Kansas City, MO 64108
816/221-1920

Negro League Baseball Players Association
425 Park Avenue, Suite 16-24
New York, NY 10022
212/874-3228 or 212/836-8072

National Baseball Hall of Fame
P.O. Box 590
Cooperstown, NY 13326
607/547-9988

Index